Asset Pricing in Discrete Time

Asset Pricing in Discrete Time
A Complete Markets Approach

SER-HUANG POON

and

RICHARD C. STAPLETON

OXFORD
UNIVERSITY PRESS

OXFORD
UNIVERSITY PRESS

Great Clarendon Street, Oxford OX2 6DP

Oxford University Press is a department of the University of Oxford.
It furthers the University's objective of excellence in research, scholarship,
and education by publishing worldwide in

Oxford New York

Auckland Bangkok Buenos Aires Cape Town Chennai
Dar es Salaam Delhi Hong Kong Istanbul Karachi Kolkata
Kuala Lumpur Madrid Melbourne Mexico City Mumbai Nairobi
São Paulo Shanghai Taipei Tokyo Toronto

Oxford is a registered trade mark of Oxford University Press
in the UK and in certain other countries

Published in the United States
by Oxford University Press Inc., New York

© Ser-Huang Poon and Richard C. Stapleton, 2005

The moral rights of the author have been asserted
Database right Oxford University Press (maker)

First published 2005

British Library Cataloguing in Publication Data

Data available

Library of Congress Cataloging in Publication Data

Data available

ISBN 0-19-927144-5

1 3 5 7 9 10 8 6 4 2

Typeset by Newgen Imaging Systems (P) Ltd., Chennai, India
Printed in Great Britain
on acid-free paper by
Biddles Ltd., King's Lynn, Norfolk

To

Ser-Huang's Husband, John

and

Dick Stapleton's Wife, Linda

ACKNOWLEDGEMENTS

We would like to thank the following colleagues, whose ideas have been incorporated in this book. Marti Subrahmanyam together with Dick Stapleton, jointly developed much of the material incorporated in Chapters 1, 3, 5, and 6. Parts of Chapter 6 rely heavily on the paper published in *Econometrica*, 1978. Guenter Franke is largely responsible for many of the original ideas in Chapters 2 and 4, published in the *Journal of Economic Theory*, 1998 and the *European Finance Review*, 1999. Chapter 6 also relies on joint work with Steven Satchell, published in the *Australian Journal of Management*, 1997. Dick Stapleton's PhD students Antonio Camara and James Huang are also jointly responsible for many of the ideas in Chapters 3 and 4. Classes of PhD students at the European Institute for Advanced Studies in Management, and at the Universities of Melbourne, Canberra, Oslo, Lancaster, Strathclyde, and Manchester have studied the material in the book and given us numerous comments. We would also like to thank Harris Schlesinger, Kristian Rydquist, and Frank Milne who read early drafts of the manuscript and Guenter Franke for detailed comments on several chapters.

PREFACE

This book covers the pricing of assets, derivatives and bonds in a discrete time, complete markets framework. It relies heavily on the existence, in a complete market, of a pricing kernel. It is primarily aimed at advanced masters and PhD students in finance. Chapter 1 deals with asset pricing in a single-period model. It derives a simple complete market pricing model and then uses Stein's lemma to derive a version of the capital asset pricing model. Chapter 2 then looks more deeply into some of the utility determinants of the pricing kernel. In particular, it investigates the effect of non-marketable background risks on the shape of the pricing kernel. Chapter 3 derives the prices of European-style contingent claims, in particular call options, in a single-period model. The Black–Scholes model is derived assuming a lognormal distribution for the asset and a pricing kernel with constant elasticity. It emphasises the idea of a risk-neutral valuation relationship (RNVR) between the price of a contingent claim on an asset and the underlying asset price. Chapter 4 extends the analysis to contingent claims on assets with non-lognormal distributions and considers the pricing of claims when RNVRs do not exist. Chapter 5 extends the treatment of asset pricing to a multi-period economy. It derives prices in a rational expectations equilibrium. The rational expectations framework is then used in Chapter 6 to analyse the pricing of forward and futures contracts on assets and derivatives. Finally, Chapter 7 extends the analysis to the pricing of bonds given stochastic interest rates. This methodology is then used to model the drift of forward rates, and as a special case the drift of the forward London Interbank Offer Rate in the LIBOR market model.

CONTENTS

1

ASSET PRICES IN A SINGLE-PERIOD MODEL

This chapter derives asset prices in a one-period model. We derive a version of the capital asset pricing model (CAPM) using a complete market, state-contingent claims approach. We define the forward pricing kernel and then use the assumption of joint normality of the cash flows and Stein's lemma to establish the CAPM. We then derive the pricing kernel in an equilibrium representative investor model.

1.1 Initial Setup and Key Assumptions

In this section we establish the value of a firm j which generates a cash flow x_j at a single point in time. There are $j = 1, 2, \ldots, J$ firms in the economy and the sum total of the cash flows $x_m = x_1 + x_2 + \cdots + x_J$, is the aggregate, or market cash flow. In the model, states of the world are represented by outcomes of the cash flows of the firms. We make the following assumptions:

1. We assume a single period extending from time t to time $t + T$. Each firm pays a dividend equal to its cash flow at $t + T$.
2. Next, we assume that forward parity holds. Since no dividends are paid between t and $t + T$, this means that the spot price $S_{j,t}$ of asset j is given by

$$S_{j,t} = F_{j,t,t+T} B_{t,t+T}, \tag{1.1}$$

   where $B_{t,t+T}$ is the price at t of a zero-coupon bond paying \$1 at time $t + T$ and $F_{j,t,t+T}$ is the forward price at time t for the delivery of asset j at time $t + T$. Note that, if this equality does not hold (i.e. forward parity is violated), arbitrage profits can be obtained by trading S, F, and B.

3. We assume that there are a finite number of states of the world at time $t + T$, indexed by $i = 1, 2, \ldots, I$, each with a positive probability of occurring. Let p_i be the probability of state i occurring. A state-contingent claim on state i is defined as a security which pays \$1 if and only if state i occurs.

4. We now assume that the markets are complete. Specifically, we assume that it is possible to buy a state-contingent claim with a forward price q_i for state i.[1] In complete markets, the q_i prices exist, for all states i.[2]

5. Assume that the investors have homogeneous expectations. This means that they agree on the probability of a state occurring and on the cash flow of each firm in each state.

6. Assume that the price of a portfolio (or a package) of contingent claims is equal to the sum of the prices of the individual state-contingent claims.[3] It follows that an asset j, which has a time $t + T$ payoff $x_{j,t+T,i}$ in the state i, has a forward price

$$F_{j,t,t+T} = \sum_i q_i x_{j,t+T,i}. \qquad (1.2)$$

For simplicity, when there is no ambiguity, we drop the time subscripts and write $F_j = \sum_i (q_i x_{j,i})$.

We will show that the above set of assumptions is sufficient to establish the pricing of assets. However, other sets of assumptions are possible. For example Pliska (1997) assumes, at a more fundamental level, just the absence of arbitrage in financial

---

[1] In practice, it may not be possible to directly purchase such state-contingent claims. However, if put and call option contracts on an asset can be purchased at all strike prices, then effectively a complete market exists for claims on the asset. Portfolios of puts and call can be formed to replicate the contingent-claim payoffs.

[2] The assumption of a finite state space could be relaxed to permit an infinite state space, while retaining the complete markets assumption. For such a generalisation, see the proof in Nachman (1982), where he assumes digital options are traded at all strike prices.

[3] This is an implication of what is known as the Law of One Price, see for example Cochrane (2001), chapter 4, or Pliska (1997), chapter 1.

markets. LeRoy and Werner (2001), equivalently, assume that a
set of assets exists which span the state space.

1.2   Properties of the State Price, q_i

We first establish some important properties of the state forward prices. Note first that q is a pricing function. We can write
$q_i = q(i)$, where convenient, to emphasise this fact. We have:

1. The state price, q_i, is always greater than zero.
   Since q_i represents the price of a claim which pays \$1 if
   a state with positive probability occurs, it is a claim with
   positive utility and thus must have a positive price, i.e.
   $q_i > 0$.

2. The state prices sum to 1, i.e. $\sum_i q_i = 1$.
   To prove that $\sum_i q_i = 1$, we use the relation in equation
   (1.2). If x_j is a certain cash flow, for example the payoff
   on a zero-coupon bond, $x_{j,i} = \$1$ for all i. In this case, the
   forward price must be equal to \$1, which means from (1.2)
   that $F_j = \sum_i 1 \cdot q_i = 1$ or $\sum_i q_i = 1$.

A set $\{q_i\}$ which is positive and sums to unity is a 'probability'
measure. Note that it is similar in many respects to the set
of probabilities $\{p_i\}$ which is also positive and sums to unity.
In the literature, q_i is often referred to as the risk-neutral
measure.[4]

1.3   A Simplification of the State Space

So far, we have defined the state space as the product of the states
of all the individual firms in the economy. We now simplify the
state space, defining the states of the world by different outcomes
of x_m, the aggregate market cash flow.

We first illustrate the state space assumed so far, using an
example with just two firms and three states for each cash flow. In
Fig. 1.1, there are three states for each firm and nine in all. These
result in nine different states for the market portfolio. Note that
firm 2 can be regarded as the combination of all the other firms in
the economy.

---

[4] For further reading on risk-neutral measures, see Williams (1991).

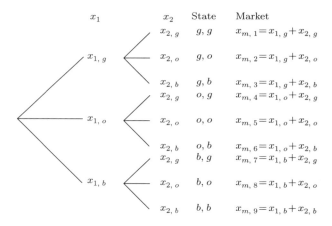

x_1	x_2	State	Market
	$x_{2,g}$	g, g	$x_{m,1} = x_{1,g} + x_{2,g}$
$x_{1,g}$	$x_{2,o}$	g, o	$x_{m,2} = x_{1,g} + x_{2,o}$
	$x_{2,b}$	g, b	$x_{m,3} = x_{1,g} + x_{2,b}$
	$x_{2,g}$	o, g	$x_{m,4} = x_{1,o} + x_{2,g}$
$x_{1,o}$	$x_{2,o}$	o, o	$x_{m,5} = x_{1,o} + x_{2,o}$
	$x_{2,b}$	o, b	$x_{m,6} = x_{1,o} + x_{2,b}$
	$x_{2,g}$	b, g	$x_{m,7} = x_{1,b} + x_{2,g}$
$x_{1,b}$	$x_{2,o}$	b, o	$x_{m,8} = x_{1,b} + x_{2,o}$
	$x_{2,b}$	b, b	$x_{m,9} = x_{1,b} + x_{2,b}$

FIG. 1.1. The state space

Notes:

1. Firm 1 has a cash flow $x_{1,g}$ in its good state, $x_{1,b}$ in its bad state, and $x_{1,o}$ in its OK state.
2. Firm 2 has a cash flow $x_{2,g}$ in its good state, $x_{2,b}$ in its bad state, and $x_{2,o}$ in its OK state.
3. There are 9 states in all, indicated by (g, g), $(g, o), \ldots, (b, b)$.
4. The market cash flow in state 1 is $x_{m,1} = x_{1,g} + x_{2,g}$, and is $x_{m,2}$ in state 2 and so on.

1.4 The Pricing Kernel, ϕ_i

In this section we define a variable, often known as the pricing kernel, ϕ. We then establish the essential properties of ϕ. It is defined by

$$\phi_i = \frac{q_i}{p_i},$$

i.e. it is the forward price of a state-contingent claim relative to the probability of the state occuring. It is sometimes, therefore, referred to as the 'probability deflated' state price. Note that the pricing kernel here is more precisely described as the 'forward pricing kernel', since q_i is the forward state price. Often, we will write $\phi = \phi(i)$ in functional form. The properties of ϕ_i are as follows:

1. Since $p_i > 0$ and $q_i > 0$, this means the pricing kernel ϕ_i is a positive function.

2. $E(\phi) = 1$. This follows immediately from the fact that the sum of the state prices is 1. We have

$$E(\phi) = \sum_i p_i \cdot \phi_i$$

$$= \sum_i p_i \cdot \frac{q_i}{p_i}$$

$$= \sum_i q_i = 1.$$

In Fig. 1.2, we illustrate the state prices, probabilities, and the pricing kernel using the same example introduced in Fig. 1.1. Note that there is a state price, q_i and a joint probability, p_i, for each

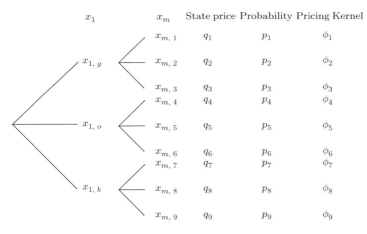

x_1	x_m	State price	Probability	Pricing Kernel
	$x_{m,1}$	q_1	p_1	ϕ_1
$x_{1,g}$	$x_{m,2}$	q_2	p_2	ϕ_2
	$x_{m,3}$	q_3	p_3	ϕ_3
	$x_{m,4}$	q_4	p_4	ϕ_4
$x_{1,o}$	$x_{m,5}$	q_5	p_5	ϕ_5
	$x_{m,6}$	q_6	p_6	ϕ_6
	$x_{m,7}$	q_7	p_7	ϕ_7
$x_{1,b}$	$x_{m,8}$	q_8	p_8	ϕ_8
	$x_{m,9}$	q_9	p_9	ϕ_9

FIG. 1.2. State space, state prices, and pricing kernel

Notes:

1. Firm 1 has a cash flow $x_{1,g}$ in its good state, $x_{1,b}$ in its bad state, and $x_{1,o}$ in its OK state.
2. Firm 2 has a cash flow $x_{2,g}$ in its good state, $x_{2,b}$ in its bad state, and $x_{2,o}$ in its OK state. x_m is the sum of x_1 and x_2.
3. There are 9 states in all of the market cash flow.
4. q_i is the state price, p_i is the probability of the state, and ϕ_i is the probability deflated state price or pricing kernel.
5. In this example, the forward price of the cash flow x_1 is given by

$$F_1 = x_{1,g}(q_1 + q_2 + q_3) + x_{1,o}(q_4 + q_5 + q_6) + x_{1,b}(q_7 + q_8 + q_9).$$

joint outcome of the firm cash flow and the market portfolio. This illustrates one potential problem. There is nothing to prevent two of the outcomes leading to the same value of x_m. In this case we will assume that the pricing kernel has the same value in both states. Note that although the state prices will not usually be the same, it is reasonable to assume that the probability deflated state prices are the same.[5] In this case we can write the pricing kernel as a function of the aggregate cash flow, i.e., $\phi = \phi(x_m)$.

Given our definition of the pricing kernel, we find, rewriting equation (1.2), that the forward price of the asset j is

$$F_j = \sum_i x_{j,i} q_i = \sum_i p_i \left[\phi(x_{m,i}) x_{j,i}\right] = E\left[\phi(x_m) x_j\right]. \qquad (1.3)$$

It follows that the case where $\phi_i = 1$, for all i, is of particular significance. In this case we would have:

$$F_j = \sum_i q_i x_{j,i}$$
$$= \sum_i p_i x_{j,i}$$
$$= E\left(x_j\right).$$

Here, the forward price equals the expected value of the cash flow. This occurs if the cash flow can be priced under the assumption of risk neutrality. Hence the case where $\phi_i = 1$, for all i, equates to the case of risk neutrality.

In order to appreciate the importance of the pricing kernel, consider the following expansion of equation (1.3). Using the definition of covariance, the forward price is[6]

$$F_j = E\left[x_j \phi(x_m)\right]$$
$$= E\left[\phi(x_m)\right] E\left(x_j\right) + \text{cov}[\phi(x_m), x_j],$$

---

[5] If deflated state prices depend upon the marginal utility for consumption in a state, as in the equilibrium model derived later, then they will depend on aggregate market cash flows rather than on the composition of the aggregate cash flow.

[6] See Exercise 1(a). The covariance between two variables X and Y is given by
$$\text{cov}(X,Y) = E\{[X - E(X)][Y - E(Y)]\}.$$

and given that $E\left[\phi(x_m)\right] = 1$, we have

$$F_j = E\left(x_j\right) + \text{cov}[\phi(x_m), x_j].$$

It follows that the behaviour of ϕ, in particular its covariance with the cash flow x_j, determines the risk premium for the asset, which is represented by the excess of the expected value of the cash flow over its forward price. In most cases, as we will see in Chapter 2, it turns out that $\phi(x_m)$ is negatively correlated with x_j, in which case the risk premium is positive.

1.5   The Capital Asset Pricing Model

In this section, we illustrate the generality of the pricing kernel approach by deriving a version of the CAPM. The CAPM can be derived either by assuming that the pricing kernel is a linear function of x_m, or by assuming that the firm's cash flow and the aggregate market cash flow are joint-normally distributed. Here we take the latter approach.

Assume that the function $\phi(x_m)$ is differentiable with $\phi'(x_m) < 0$, as in Fig. 1.3 and that x_j, x_m are joint-normally distributed. It then follows from Stein's lemma (see appendix at the end of the book) that:

$$F_j = E\left(x_j\right) E\left[\phi(x_m)\right] - \kappa \, \text{cov}(x_j, x_m).$$
$$= E\left(x_j\right) - \kappa \, \text{cov}(x_j, x_m), \tag{1.4}$$

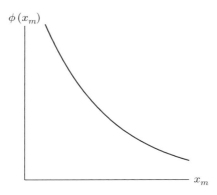

FIG. 1.3. The pricing kernel

since $E[\phi(x_m)] = 1$, where

$$\kappa = -E[\phi'(x_m)].$$

This is a cash flow version of the well-known CAPM. The more familiar rate of return version of the CAPM follows in a few steps from (1.4).

First, we apply the model to find the forward price of the market cash flow, x_m. This is given by

$$F_m = E(x_m) - \kappa \operatorname{var}(x_m), \tag{1.5}$$

where F_m is the forward price of the market portfolio cash flow, x_m. Rearranging (1.5), we get the market price of risk,

$$\kappa = \frac{-F_m + E(x_m)}{\operatorname{var}(x_m)}. \tag{1.6}$$

The forward price of asset j is then, substituting in (1.4),

$$F_j = E(x_j) - \left[\frac{-F_m + E(x_m)}{\operatorname{var}(x_m)}\right] \operatorname{cov}(x_m, x_j).$$

Dividing both sides by the forward price, F_j, we obtain

$$1 = \frac{E(x_j)}{F_j} - \left[\frac{E(x_m) - F_m}{\operatorname{var}(x_m)}\right] \operatorname{cov}\left(x_m, \frac{x_j}{F_j}\right).$$

Rearranging this equation gives

$$\frac{E(x_j) - F_j}{F_j} = \left[\frac{E(x_m) - F_m}{F_m}\right] \frac{\operatorname{cov}(x_m/F_m, x_j/F_j)}{\operatorname{var}(x_m/F_m)}. \tag{1.7}$$

Finally, if we denote $\beta_j = \operatorname{cov}(x_m/F_m, x_j/F_j)/\operatorname{var}(x_m/F_m)$ as the beta of x_j with respect to the market portfolio, then,

$$\frac{E(x_j) - F_j}{F_j} = \beta_j \left[\frac{E(x_m) - F_m}{F_m}\right].$$

This is a forward version of the standard CAPM. It says that the risk premium of a stock is the beta of the stock times the risk premium on the market.

Now, in order to derive the more familiar spot version of the CAPM, substitute the forward price $F_j = S_j(1 + r_f)$, using spot-forward parity, where $B^{-1}_{t,t+T} = (1 + r_f)$ and let S_m be the spot value of the market portfolio. Then, we have:

$$\frac{E(x_j)}{S_j} - (1 + r_f) = \beta_j \left[\frac{E(x_m)}{S_m} - (1 + r_f) \right].$$

Finally, denoting the returns on S_j and S_m as r_j and r_m, respectively, we find that

$$E(r_j) - r_f = \beta_j \left[E(r_m) - r_f \right].$$

This is the more commonly seen spot version of the CAPM.

1.6 The Arbitrage Pricing Theory

In this section we apply the pricing kernel approach to derive a version of the arbitrage pricing theory (APT). We assume that the cash flow of firm j, x_j is a linear function of a set of factors. For example, we assume there are K factors and for factor f_k the factor loading is β_{jk}. In this case

$$x_j = a_j + \sum_{k=1}^{K} \beta_{jk} f_k + \varepsilon_j,$$

where ε_j is independent of f_k. We then have:

$$\text{cov}[x_j, \phi(x_m)] = \sum_{k=1}^{K} \beta_{jk} \text{cov}[f_k, \phi(x_m)] + \text{cov}[\varepsilon_j, \phi(x_m)].$$

Note that this is merely an expansion of the covariance term into K covariances with the underlying factors, plus a residual covariance. However, if one of the following conditions holds, an economically meaningful decomposition follows. The conditions are:

(i) there is no idiosyncratic risk, $\varepsilon_j = 0$; or
(ii) the idiosyncratic risk is not related to the pricing kernel, $\text{cov}[\varepsilon_j, \phi(x_m)] = 0$.

If $\varepsilon_j = 0$ or $\text{cov}[\varepsilon_j, \phi(x_m)] = 0$, then

$$\text{cov}[x_j, \phi(x_m)] = \sum_{k=1}^{K} \beta_{jk} \text{cov}[f_k, \phi(x_m)]$$

$$F_j = E(x_j) + \beta_{j1}\text{cov}[f_1, \phi(x_m)] + \beta_{j2}\text{cov}[f_2, \phi(x_m)] + \cdots.$$

Here, the risk premium $E(x_j) - F_j$ is the sum of K risk premia.

This is a version of the APT model. Note that the APT is a paradigm which is somewhat different from the CAPM. For the CAPM we need either quadratic utility or the joint-normal distribution. These assumptions are not required for the APT provided that $\text{cov}[\varepsilon_j, \phi(x_m)] = 0$ or $\varepsilon_j = 0$. In other words; (i) idiosyncratic risk is not priced; or (ii) x_j is a fully diversified portfolio.

1.7   Risk Aversion and the Pricing Kernel in an Equilibrium Model

So far we have worked with the pricing kernel ϕ_i, with no underlying model of the determinants of this crucial variable. We now derive one such model. Equilibrium models assume that investors maximise expected utility and derive an equilibrium in which markets clear, i.e. there is zero excess demand for all assets. In this section, we simplify the model somewhat, by assuming that there is only one investor in the economy. An alternative, equivalent assumption is that the market acts as if there is just one investor with 'average' characteristics. This is often referred to as the 'representative agent' assumption.[7]

Let $w_{t+T,i}$ be the wealth of the investor in the state i at time $t + T$. Assume that the investor is endowed with investible wealth w_t at time t, in the form of cash. The investor can purchase state-contingent claims which pay \$1, if and only if the state i occurs at time $t + T$. The price of the claims are q_i for $i = 1, 2, \ldots, I$. The investor's problem is to choose a set of state-contingent claims paying $w_{t+T,i}$, given a budget allocation of cash, w_t.

We make the following additional assumptions:

1. The investor maximises the expected value of a utility function $u(w_{t+T})$. Hence the investors problem is:

$$\max_{w_{t+T,i}} E\left[u\left(w_{t+T}\right)\right] = \sum_i p_i \, u(w_{t+T,i})$$

   subject to

$$\sum_i w_{t+T,i} \, q_i \, B_{t,t+T} = w_t. \tag{1.8}$$

2. The utility function has the properties $u'(w_{t+T}) > 0$ (non-satiation) and $u''(w_{t+T}) < 0$ (risk aversion).

---

[7] See, for example, Huang and Litzenberger (1988), Chapter 5.

The first assumption follows from the more basic assumption of rational choice.[8] The second assumption guarantees that satisfying the first-order conditions leads to an optimal and unique solution. Note that the discount factor enters the budget constraint because the q_i are forward prices, whereas the given cash wealth w_t is a time t allocation.

We solve the optimisation problem by forming the Lagrangian:

$$L = \sum_i p_i \, u(w_{t+T,i}) + \lambda \left[w_t B_{t,t+T}^{-1} - \sum_i q_i \, w_{t+T,i} \right].$$

Then the first-order conditions for a maximum are:

$$\frac{\partial L}{\partial w_{t+T,i}} = p_i \, u'(w_{t+T,i}) - q_i \lambda = 0. \tag{1.9}$$

Summing equation (1.9) over the states i we then find

$$\sum_i p_i \, u'(w_{t+T,i}) = \lambda \sum_i q_i$$

or

$$E[u'(w_{t+T})] = \lambda,$$

since $\sum_i q_i = 1$. Now, substituting for λ in (1.9), the first-order condition becomes

$$\frac{p_i \, u'(w_{t+T,i})}{E[u'(w_{t+T})]} = q_i,$$

or

$$\phi_i = \frac{q_i}{p_i} = \frac{u'(w_{t+T,i})}{E[u'(w_{t+T})]}.$$

In this model, a condition for the investor's expected utility to be maximised is that the pricing kernel equals the ratio of marginal utility in a state to the expected marginal utility. To complete the model, we need to determine the investor's wealth at time $t+T$, in each state. However, in equilibrium the

---

[8] This follows from the Von Neuman–Morgenstern expected utility theorem, see Fama and Miller (1972). Basically, it states that if the investor behaves according to five axioms of choice under uncertainty, then maximising expected utility should always lead to maximising utility and hence to an optimal investment choice. The five axioms govern the comparability, transivity, independence, certainty equivalence, and ranking of choices.

single investor's demand for state-contingent claims must equal the available supply. Hence $w_{t+T,i}$ must equal $x_{m,i}$, the aggregate market cash flow in, state i. Substituting in the expression for the pricing kernel, we conclude that

$$\phi_i = \frac{u'(x_{m,i})}{E[u'(x_{m,i})]},$$

for all i. Hence, we have

$$\phi = \phi(x_m),$$

as assumed earlier in the chapter. Since marginal utility is a positive function of x_m and we may assume $u''(x_m) < 0$, it follows that $\phi(x_m)$ is a declining function of x_m as assumed in Fig. 1.3.

1.8   Examples

1.8.1   *Case 1: Risk Neutrality*

A risk-neutral investor is one who has a linear utility function

$$u(w_{t+T}) = a + b\,w_{t+T},$$

where a and b are constants. Then differentiating the utility function

$$u'(w_{t+T}) = E[u'(w_{t+T})] = b$$

and the pricing kernel is therefore

$$\phi_i(w_{i,t+T}) = \frac{u'(w_{i,t+T})}{E[u'(w_{t+T})]} = 1.$$

In this case, the forward price is

$$F_{t,t+T} = E(\phi\,x) = E(1 \cdot x) = E(F_{t+T,t+T}).$$

In this example of risk neutrality, $F_{t,t+T} = E(F_{t+T,t+T})$ has the martingale property.

1.8.2   *Case 2: Utility is Quadratic*

Assume utility is given by:

$$u(w_{t+T}) = a + bw_{t+T} + \delta w_{t+T}^2,$$

where $b > 0$, $\delta < 0$. In this case, marginal utility is

$$u'(w_{t+T}) = b + 2\delta w_{t+T}, \quad u' > 0$$

and the pricing kernel is given by

$$\phi(w_{t+T}) = \frac{u'(w_{t+T})}{E[u'(w_{t+T})]}$$

$$= \frac{b + 2\delta w_{t+T}}{b + 2\delta E(w_{t+T})}.$$

We then have

$$\text{cov}[\phi(w_{t+T}), x_{j,t+T}] = \frac{2\delta \text{cov}(w_{t+T}, x_{j,t+T})}{b + 2\delta E(w_{t+T})},$$

and the forward price of $x_{j,t+T}$ is

$$F_{j,t,t+T} = E(x_{j,t+T}) + \kappa \, \text{cov}(w_{t+T}, x_{j,t+T}), \qquad (1.10)$$

where

$$\kappa = \frac{2\delta}{b + 2\delta E(w_{t+T})}$$

is a constant. Equation (1.10) is a version of the CAPM. Earlier, the CAPM was derived under the assumption that wealth and asset prices were joint normal. This example illustrates that quadratic utility is an alternative sufficient condition. In this case, the pricing kernel is linear in wealth.

1.9 A Note on the Equivalent Martingale Measure

We noted above that the set of forward state prices $\{q_i\}$ is a probability measure. In the literature it is often referred to as the *Equivalent Martingale Measure*, or simply EMM. Since this measure will be used extensively in later chapters, we now include a brief explanation of this terminology.

Let $P = \{p_i\}$ and $Q = \{q_i\}$ be two probability measures. P and Q are equivalent if $q_i > 0$ if and only if $p_i > 0$. Let $E^P(.)$ and $E^Q(.)$ be expectations under the probability measures, P and Q, respectively. From equation (1.2), dropping the j subscript:

$$F = \sum_i q_i x_i = E^Q(x)$$

$$= \sum_i p_i(\phi_i x_i) = E^P(\phi x).$$

Now rewrite the forward price, F, as $F_{t,t+T}$. Also, note that the time $t + T$ spot price, x, can be expressed as $F_{t+T,t+T}$. This is because the forward price at $t+T$ for immediate delivery, is simply the spot price at $t + T$. Hence

$$F_{t,t+T} = E^Q\left(F_{t+T,t+T}\right).$$

If such a relationship holds, the variable is said to have the Martingale property, and Q is therefore referred to as the EMM.[9] In the literature, E^Q is often used loosely as the risk-neutral measure, since it has the same property that the true measure would have under risk neutrality, the case discussed in Section 1.8.1.

1.10   A Note on the Asset Specific Pricing Kernel, $\psi(x_j)$

The asset specific pricing kernel was introduced by Brennan (1979) and is important in the analysis of option pricing. It is the expected value of the pricing kernel $\phi(x_m)$ given the outcome of x_j. For asset j, we can write the forward price

$$F_j = \mathop{E}_{x,\phi}\left[\phi(x_m)x_j\right] = \mathop{E}_{x}\left\{\mathop{E}_{\phi}\left[\phi(x_m) \mid x_j\right]x_j\right\},$$

where the notation $\mathop{E}_{x}$ indicates expectation over values of x. Defining $\psi(x_j) = \mathop{E}_{\phi}\left[\phi(x_m) \mid x_j\right]$, we have

$$F_j = \mathop{E}_{x}\left[\psi(x_j)x_j\right].$$

Two properties of the asset-specific pricing kernel are important and will be used in later chapters. First, it follows directly from $\phi(x_m) > 0$, that $\psi(x_j) > 0$. Second, $E[\psi(x_j)] = 1$. This property follows from the fact that the forward price of a non-stochastic cash flow, must be the the cash flow itself. Alternatively, directly we have

$$\mathop{E}_{x}\left\{\mathop{E}_{\phi}\left[\phi(x_m) \mid x_j\right]\right\} = E[\phi(x_m)] = 1.$$

---

[9] The concept of EMM and the use of this probability measure were made popular by Harrison and Krepps (1979). For a detailed discussion see Williams (1991).

1.11 Conclusions

We have used a complete markets approach to derive asset forward prices in a one-period model. Readers can compare our approach to that of other well-known texts on financial theory. It is closely related to the model developed by Huang and Litzenberger (1988). However, for the most part our approach does not require an equilibrium, although such an equilibrium could be one possible way for the pricing kernel to be determined. The CAPM derived in this chapter is incomplete in one respect. Under the assumption of joint normality we have derived a linear relationship between the risk premium on the stock and the risk premium on the market. However, unless we have an equilibrium model, we do not know that the risk premium on the market is positive.

Our use of the pricing kernel is similar in many respects to the use of a 'stochastic discount factor' in Cochrane (2001). However, as in Huang and Litzenberger (1988), the emphasis in Cochrane is on a consumption based CAPM. Our approach is closer to that used by Pliska (1997). The difference is that Pliska starts at the more basic level of a no-arbitrage economy. His more mathematical treatment is targeted at deriving prices in incomplete markets.

Exercises

1.1. (a) Use the definition of covariance to show that
$$E\left(xy\right) = E\left(x\right)E\left(y\right) + \mathrm{cov}(x, y).$$
(b) Show, using a numerical example, that
$$E\left(xy\right) = E\left[xE\left(y \,|\, x\right)\right].$$

1.2. Assume there are 3 states with probabilities $(0.3, 0.4, 0.3)$. Suppose the corresponding state prices are $(0.36, 0.38, 0.26)$. Illustrate the probability distribution of the pricing kernel.

1.3. Assume the following joint probability distribution of (x, ϕ) :

x	ϕ			
	0.6	0.8	1.2	1.4
10	0.4	0.1	0	0
5	0	0	0.1	0.4

Compute the forward price of the asset using $F = E\left(\phi x\right)$ and using $F = E\left[xE\left(\phi \,|\, x\right)\right]$.

1.4. Show that the pricing kernel in an economy of risk-neutral investors is always 1 and in this economy $E^P = E^Q$.

1.5. Assume that utility is cubic:
$$u\left(w_{t+T}\right) = a + bw_{t+T} + \delta w_{t+T}^2 + \gamma w_{t+T}^3.$$
Compute ϕ and $\mathrm{cov}(\phi, x)$, and derive a CAPM relating the forward price, F, to the expected payoff, $E\left(x\right)$.

1.6. Explain the significance of each of the assumptions made in section 1.1. Which of the assumptions is strong in the sense of 'not being likely to be true in practice'. How could the theory be generalised by relaxing these assumptions?

1.7. Assume that three firms produce cash flows: x_1, x_2, x_3 each with possible outcomes $(1, 0)$, with probability 0.5 and assume the cash flows are independent. Assume that the pricing kernel, $\phi(x_m)$ has the following values, $\phi(0) = 1.8$, $\phi(1) = 1.2$, $\phi(2) = 0.8$, $\phi(3) = 0.2$:
(a) Show the distribution of q_i.
(b) Show that $E(\phi) = 1$.
(c) Compute the forward price of cash flow x_1.

1.8. Assume that an investor has power utility with

$$u'(w) = \left(\frac{w}{1 - \gamma}\right)^{\gamma - 1},$$

with $\gamma < 1, \gamma \neq 0$.

Assume that there are only three states of the world, $i = 1, 2, 3$. Write out the maximisation of expected utility problem for the investor. Show the first-order conditions for a maximum.

2

RISK AVERSION, BACKGROUND RISK, AND THE PRICING KERNEL

We have seen in Chapter 1 that asset prices depend on the characteristics of the pricing kernel, $\phi(x_m)$. In the simple case, where all investors are identical, we can model the pricing kernel using the utility function of the 'representative investor'. In this chapter we look in more detail at utility functions and their effect on the shape of the pricing kernel. We discuss the meaning of risk aversion, in particular 'relative risk aversion' and show that if relative risk aversion is constant at different levels of wealth, then the pricing kernel exhibits constant elasticity. We then show that the introduction of 'background risk', i.e., non-hedgeable risks, causes the pricing kernel to exhibit declining elasticity. This effect on the pricing kernel is particularly significant for the pricing of options.

2.1 Risk Aversion and Declining Marginal Utility of Wealth

Consider the well-known St. Petersburg Paradox (Bernoulli, 1738) that describes the probability game where one tosses a coin till a head is obtained. The game offers the investor \$1 if a head is obtained on the first toss, \$2 if the head is first obtained on the second, \$4 if head is first obtained on the third, \$8 on the fourth, and so on. If the game consists of n possible tosses, the expected value of the game is

$$(0.5)\,(\$1) + (0.5)^2\,(\$2) + (0.5)^3\,(\$4) + \cdots + (0.5)^n\,(\$2^{n-1}) = \frac{\$n}{2}.$$

Now assume that $n \to \infty$, i.e., there is no limit on the number of tosses of the coin. The expected payoff from the game is infinite. However, although the expected value of the game is infinite, reasonable individuals would be willing to pay at most a few dollars to play a game with an expected payoff of infinity. One possible explanation is that most investors are risk averse. The amount that a risk averse individual will pay is less than the expected return of the game, since risk represents a source of disutility.

The utility of wealth, describes the level of satisfaction gained from a given amount of wealth. A utility function defines the relationship between the amount of wealth and the utility the investor derives from it. There are some commonly accepted characteristics of utility functions. *Insatiability* means individual will prefer more wealth to less, i.e., the first derivative of the utility function is positive. *Diminishing marginal utility* means the additional utility derived from an additional unit of wealth decreases as wealth increases, i.e., the second derivative of utility function is negative.

We will assume that an individual's utility function for wealth $u(w)$ is three times differentiable, i.e., the derivatives $u'(w)$, $u''(w)$, and $u'''(w)$ exist. A rational investor is averse to risk if $u'(w) > 0$ and $u''(w) < 0$. This is the case where the marginal utility of wealth is positive and declining. Such an investor will decline to participate in a fair game. The general shape of the utility function is illustrated in Fig. 2.1.

As an example, assume that an investor has a utility function:

$$u(w) = w^\gamma,$$

with $0 < \gamma < 1$. This utility function has the properties:

$$u'(w) = \gamma w^{\gamma-1} > 0,$$

$$u''(w) = \gamma(\gamma - 1)w^{\gamma-2} < 0.$$

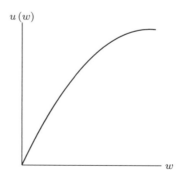

FIG. 2.1. Positive, declining marginal utility

Assume that this investor faces a fair gamble of w_0 in return for $(w_0 + \varepsilon)$ with probability $p = 0.5$, and $(w_0 - \varepsilon)$ with probability $1\text{-}p = 0.5$. The expected value of the incremental utility from taking the gamble is

$$E[u(\varepsilon)] = 0.5(w_0 + \varepsilon)^\gamma + 0.5(w_0 - \varepsilon)^\gamma - w_0^\gamma.$$

Differentiating with respect to ϵ, we find

$$\frac{\partial E[u(\varepsilon)]}{\partial \varepsilon} = 0.5\gamma(w_0 + \varepsilon)^{\gamma - 1} - 0.5\gamma(w_0 - \varepsilon)^{\gamma - 1} < 0.$$

The investor faces an expected reduction in utility if he or she accepts a gamble with $\varepsilon \neq 0$. This is because of the non-linearity (i.e., convexity) of the utility function. In this example if we assume, as in Chapter 1, that the investor maximises the expected utility of wealth, then the fair gamble will be rejected.

2.2 Absolute Risk Aversion

One of the frequently encountered assumptions in finance is that investors have exponential utility functions. Here we assume that the representative investor has an exponential utility function of the form:

$$u\left(w\right) = A - e^{-\alpha w}.$$

It follows that

$$u'(w) = \alpha e^{-\alpha w} > 0,$$

$$u''(w) = -\alpha^2 e^{-\alpha w} < 0.$$

We now explore the implications of this function for the risk premium. First, for the representative investor, wealth $w = x_m$, the aggregate cash flow of the firms in the economy. In the previous chapter we found that, under the assumption of normality, the risk premium for a cash flow was proportionate to $E[\phi'(x_m)]$, where

$$\phi(x_m) = \frac{u'(x_m)}{E[u'(x_m)]}.$$

Evaluating this expression in the case of exponential utility we have:

$$E[\phi'(x_m)] = \frac{E[u''(x_m)]}{E[u'(x_m)]} = \frac{-\alpha^2 E[e^{-\alpha x}]}{\alpha E[e^{-\alpha x}]} = -\alpha,$$

a constant. Hence, in the context of the CAPM, exponential utility is of central importance. If the representative investor has exponential utility, the market price of risk, $E[\phi'(x_m)]$, is non-stochastic. We will use this property in Chapter 5, when deriving a tractable multi-period asset pricing model.

The above property of exponential utility is closely related to the fact that for this function

$$-\frac{u''(w)}{u'(w)} = \frac{\alpha^2 e^{-\alpha w}}{\alpha e^{-\alpha w}} = \alpha.$$

In general, for any utility function, the ratio $a(w) = -u''(w)/u'(w)$ is known as the *coefficient of absolute risk aversion*. The degree of risk aversion is measured by $a(w)$. In the case of exponential utility, $a(w) = \alpha$, a constant. However, for utility functions other than the exponential, $a(w)$ is stochastic and dependent on wealth. For this reason exponential utility is often referred to as *Constant Absolute Risk Aversion* utility, or CARA.

The degree of absolute risk aversion also determines the changes in the *absolute* amount of risky investment an investor will make as wealth increases. Absolute risk aversion could be decreasing, constant or increasing. If the investor increases the absolute amount invested in risky assets as his or her wealth increases, then the investor is said to exhibit decreasing absolute risk aversion.

In practice, one would expect, for most investors, that as wealth increases the dollar amount invested in risky assets will increase. This explains why declining absolute risk aversion is a commonly made assumption. This assumption restricts the possible utility function that could describe the investor's preferences to a reasonable set.[10]

2.2.1 *Relative Risk Aversion*

Another frequently encountered utility function is the power function. The most convenient form of this function is as follows:

$$u(w) = \frac{1-\gamma}{\gamma}\left(\frac{w}{1-\gamma}\right)^{\gamma},$$

---

[10] Pratt (1964) shows that when two investors, indexed as 1 and 2, are facing the choice of investment in one risky and one risk-free asset and if $a_1(w) > a_2(w)$, investor 1 will invest less money in the risky asset than investor 2, regardless of his/her level of wealth.

where γ is a constant such that

$$\gamma < 1, \quad \text{and} \quad \gamma \neq 0.$$

Taking the first derivative:

$$u'(w) = \left(\frac{w}{1-\gamma}\right)^{\gamma-1}.$$

Further,

$$u''(w) = \frac{\gamma-1}{1-\gamma}\left(\frac{w}{1-\gamma}\right)^{\gamma-2},$$

and the coefficient of absolute risk aversion is

$$a(w) = -\frac{u''(w)}{u'(w)} = \frac{1-\gamma}{w}.$$

This is an example of declining absolute risk aversion. Further, since $a(w)$ declines in proportion to wealth, we say that the power function exhibits constant relative risk aversion (CRRA). We define the coefficient of relative risk aversion as[11]

$$r(w) = \frac{-u''(w)}{u'(w)}w.$$

In the case of the power function above, the relative risk aversion is:

$$r(w) = 1 - \gamma.$$

If the investor increases the proportionate amount invested in risky assets as wealth increases, then the investor is said to exhibit decreasing relative risk aversion. Theoretically, investors may also exhibit CRRA or increasing relative risk aversion. While there is a general agreement that most investors exhibit decreasing absolute risk aversion, there is much less agreement concerning relative or proportional risk aversion.

The importance of the power function in the context of asset pricing is illustrated below. Assuming again a representative

---

[11] Merton (1969) shows that two investors with different levels of wealth, w_1 and w_2, will invest the same proportion of their wealth in the risky asset and risk-free asset if $r_1(w) = r_2(w)$.

investor with utility $u(x_m)$, we now assume that the investor has power utility:

$$u(x_m) = \frac{1 - \gamma}{\gamma} \left(\frac{x_m}{1 - \gamma} \right)^{\gamma}.$$

It then follows that the pricing kernel in this case is

$$\phi(x_m) = \frac{u'(x_m)}{E[u'(x_m)]}$$

$$= \frac{(x_m/1 - \gamma)^{\gamma - 1}}{E\left[(x_m/1 - \gamma)^{\gamma - 1} \right]}.$$

Assume now that a cash flow, x_j and the aggregate market cash flow, x_m are joint-lognormally distributed. The logarithmic mean of x_j is $E(\ln x)$ and the logarithmic variance is $\text{var}(\ln x)$. Also, the logarithmic mean of the pricing kernel is $E(\ln \phi)$ and the logarithmic variance is $\text{var}(\ln \phi)$. If y is a lognormal variable,

$$E(y) = e^{E(\ln y) + \frac{1}{2} \text{var}(\ln y)}.$$

We then have the forward price

$$F_j = E\left[x_j \phi(x_m) \right]$$

$$= e^{E\{\ln[x_j \phi(x_m)]\} + \frac{1}{2} \text{var}\{\ln[x_j \phi(x_m)]\}},$$

where

$$E\left\{ \ln\left[x_j \phi(x_m) \right] \right\} = E\left[\ln x_j + \ln \phi(x_m) \right].$$

Now, using the relationship

$$\text{var}\left\{ \ln[x_j \phi(x_m)] \right\} = \text{var}[\ln x_j + \ln \phi(x_m)]$$

$$= \text{var}(\ln x_j) + \text{var}[\ln \phi(x_m)]$$

$$+ 2\text{cov}[\ln x_j, \ln \phi(x_m)]$$

and the property $E(\phi) = 1$, we find

$$F_j = E(x_j)e^{\text{cov}[\ln x_j, \ln \phi(x_m)]},$$

and hence

$$\frac{F_j}{E(x_j)} = e^{\text{cov}[\ln x, \ln \phi(x_m)]}.$$

Hence, using the pricing kernel:

$$\phi(x_m) = \frac{(x_m/(1-\gamma))^{\gamma-1}}{E\left[(x_m/(1-\gamma))^{\gamma-1}\right]},$$

it follows that

$$\text{cov}[\ln x_j, \ln \phi(x_m)] = (\gamma - 1)\text{cov}(\ln x_j, \ln x_m)$$

and

$$\frac{F_j}{E(x_j)} = e^{(\gamma-1)\text{cov}(\ln x_j, \ln x_m)}. \tag{2.1}$$

In this model, where the cash flows x_j and x_m are joint log-normal, and where the representative investor has power utility, the risk premium, expressed as the ratio of the forward price to the expected value of the cash flow, is a constant. In equation (2.1) γ and the covariance term are constants. This stems from the CRRA property, which implies that the risk premium is the same at all levels of the cash flow.[12]

2.2.2 The Elasticity of the Pricing Kernel

A precise measure of the degree to which the pricing kernel reflects constant or declining relative risk aversion is its elasticity. We may define the elasticity of the pricing kernel by the following relationship:

$$\nu(x_m) = -\frac{\partial \phi(x_m)/\phi(x_m)}{\partial x_m/x_m}.$$

If the representative investor has power utility, we saw above that the relative risk aversion is constant. It follows that in this case, the elasticity of the pricing kernel is constant. We have

$$\nu(x_m) = -\frac{\partial \phi(x_m)/\phi(x_m)}{\partial x_m/x_m} = \left[-\frac{u''(x_m)}{u'(x_m)}\right] x_m.$$

Hence, in the representative investor economy, the elasticity of the pricing kernel is simply the degree of relative risk aversion of the investor. Hence, in the case of the pricing kernel $\phi(x_m)$ we

---

[12] The same property implies that in inter-temporal models the proportionate risk premium is non-stochastic. See, for example, the model of Rubinstein (1976).

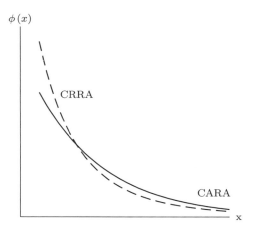

$\phi(x)$

CRRA

CARA

x

FIG. 2.2. Pricing kernel: CARA and CRRA

use the terms elasticity of the pricing kernel and the relative risk aversion of the representative investor interchangeably. However we will also discuss in Chapter 3 about the elasticity of the firm-specific pricing kernel, defined in a similar manner, using $\psi(x_j)$ rather than $\phi(x_m)$.

The elasticity of two pricing kernels is illustrated in Fig. 2.2, for the cases of CARA and CRRA. The case of CARA assumes that $u(x) = -e^{-ax}$ with $a = 0.28$. The case of CRRA assumes that $u(x) = [(1 - \gamma)/\gamma][x/(1 - \gamma)]^\gamma$ with $\gamma = -3.98$. From the graph it can be observed that the pricing kernel in the case of CRRA has the property of constant elasticity. In the case of the CARA, the elasticity is non-constant, and is in fact increasing with x.

2.2.3 *Prudence*

An important characteristic of the pricing kernel, which determines the pricing of options, is the rate of decline of its elasticity. Mathematically, this decline is determined by the third derivative of the utility function of the representative investor.[13] It is

---

[13] A positive third derivative of the utility function indicates a precautionary saving motive. It reflects how uncertainty about future income will

given by

$$\nu'(w) = -\left[\frac{u'''(w)u'(w) - u''(w)u''(w)}{u'(w)u'(w)}\right]w - \frac{u''(w)}{u'(w)}.$$

Rearranging this derivative:

$$\nu'(w) = a(w)\left\{1 - w\left[\frac{-u'''(w)}{u''(w)} - a(w)\right]\right\}.$$

Defining

$$p = \frac{-u'''(w)}{u''(w)}$$

as the absolute prudence of the utility function and $wp(w)$ as the relative prudence, we obtain

$$\nu'(w) = a(w)\left\{1 - [wp(w) - wa(w)]\right\}.$$

It follows that $\nu' < 0$ if the difference between relative prudence and relative risk aversion exceeds unity.

Note that absolute prudence is analogous to absolute risk aversion, but involves the second and third derivatives of the utility function rather than the first and second derivatives. Also the more prudent is the utility function, given the absolute risk aversion, the more the pricing kernel elasticity declines. To illustrate the calculation of absolute prudence, we take power utility as an example,

$$u(w) = w^\gamma, \quad \text{where } \gamma < 1,$$

$$a(w) = -\frac{u''(w)}{u'(w)} = \frac{-\gamma(\gamma-1)w^{\gamma-2}}{\gamma w^{\gamma-1}} = \frac{1-\gamma}{w},$$

$$p(w) = \frac{-\gamma(\gamma-1)(\gamma-2)w^{\gamma-3}}{\gamma(\gamma-1)w^{\gamma-2}} = \frac{2-\gamma}{w}.$$

reduce current consumption and investment in risky assets and increase current saving. See Kimball (1990).

Note that, in this case, absolute prudence exceeds absolute risk aversion and

$$wp(w) - wa(w) = 1,$$

which is consistent with constant elasticity.

The coefficient of absolute risk aversion, $a(w) > 0$ indicates positive risk aversion and the coefficient of absolute prudence, $p(w) > 0$ indicates positive prudence. When $a'(w) < 0$, investors become less risk averse as they get wealthier. $p'(w) < 0$ indicates declining prudence; investors become less prudent as they get wealthier. An investor is said to be *standard risk averse* if $a(w) > 0$, $a'(w) < 0$, $p(w) > 0$ and $p'(w) < 0$. The HARA class of functions, excluding the exponential utility function, are standard risk averse. The significance of standard risk aversion is as follows: a standard risk averse investor will act in a more risk averse manner towards risky assets when faced with a zero-mean, additive background risk.[14]

To illustrate non-constant elasticity of the pricing kernel, we now introduce a wider class of utility functions. Most utility functions used in Finance, are members of the hyperbolic absolute risk averse (HARA) class.

First, we define the HARA class. A HARA utility function is of the form:

$$u(w) = \frac{1 - \gamma}{\gamma} \left(\frac{A + w}{1 - \gamma} \right)^{\gamma},$$

if $\gamma \neq 0$, where A and γ are constants such that (i) $\gamma < 1$ and $A + w > 0$, or (ii) $\gamma = 2$.

If $\gamma = 0$, the HARA utility function is defined by the marginal utility function

$$u'(w) = \left(\frac{A + w}{1 - \gamma} \right)^{\gamma - 1} = \frac{1}{A + w}.$$

---

[14] For a definition of background risk, see Section 2.3. An example of a non-standard risk averse investor is one with exponential utility. Such an investor has $a'(w) = 0$ and $p'(w) = 0$. So the exponential utility investor will not react to background risk by becoming more risk averse to marketable risks.

Note that the power function (CRRA) is a special case where $A = 0$. Also $u(w) = \ln(w)$ when $A = 0$ and $\gamma = 0$.[15] Also, the exponential utility function is a special case where $\gamma \to -\infty$.

The relative risk aversion of the utility function is directly affected by the constant A. If $A < 0$ the utility function exhibits declining relative risk aversion. To see this, differentiate the marginal utility function and obtain

$$u''(w) = -\left(\frac{A+w}{1-\gamma}\right)^{\gamma-2}.$$

The relative risk aversion is hence

$$r(w) = \left(\frac{1-\gamma}{A+w}\right) w,$$

which declines in w when $A < 0$. Differentiating again,

$$u'''(w) = -\left(\frac{\gamma-2}{1-\gamma}\right)\left(\frac{A+w}{1-\gamma}\right)^{\gamma-3}.$$

The absolute prudence is then given by

$$p(w) = \frac{2-\gamma}{A+w}.$$

Also, the difference between the relative prudence and relative risk aversion is

$$\frac{w}{A+w},$$

---

[15] In the case of the logarithmic utility function, we have:

$$u(w) = \ln w,$$

$$u'(w) = \frac{1}{w},$$

$$u''(w) = -\frac{1}{w^2},$$

$$a(w) = -\left(-\frac{1}{w^2}\middle/\frac{1}{w}\right) = \frac{1}{w},$$

$$r(w) = w \times a(w) = 1.$$

Since $r(w)$ is a constant, log utility is an example of the class of Constant Relative Risk Averse utility functions. $a(w)$ is positive but $a'(w) = -1/w^2 < 0$, which means that the investor is decreasing absolute risk averse. A log utility investor is one who is myopic.

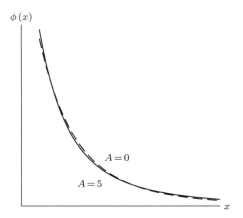

FIG. 2.3. Declining and constant elasticity

which is greater than 1 when $A < 0$, confirming that the elasticity of the pricing kernel declines when $A < 0$.

In Fig. 2.3, we illustrate the effect of the constant A factor on the elasticity of the pricing kernel. The solid line plots the pricing kernel under DRRA, with $A = -5$ and $\gamma = -2$. The dotted line plots the pricing kernel under CRRA, with $A = 0$ and $\gamma = -3.98$. The example assumes a uniform distribution for $x_m = 10, 11, \ldots, 19$ and is calibrated so that the two pricing kernels have expected values equal to unity and produce the same forward price. In both cases, $F = E[x_m \phi(x_m)] = 11.92$. Note that the two pricing kernels intersect twice.

The example illustrates the fact that two pricing kernels, calibrated to give the same forward price of an asset, one with constant relative risk aversion and one with declining relative risk aversion, must intersect twice. This is important in the valuation of options, since, as we will see in Chapter 4, the convexity of the pricing kernel is a crucial determinant of the relative pricing of options.

2.3   Background Risk and the Pricing Kernel

In this section, we analyse the effect on investors' attitudes towards marketable risky assets of a second non-hedgeable risk, such as labour income uncertainty. These secondary risks are called background risks. The CAPM, derived in Chapter 1, assumes that investors are risk averse, i.e., $u'(w) > 0$, $u''(w) < 0$ and derives an equilibrium in which the beta of a company's stock determines its cost of capital. Risk aversion implies that the pricing kernel is a declining function of aggregate wealth, $\phi'(w) = \phi'(x_m) < 0$, as shown in the analysis of the representative investor's utility. However, an individual's attitude to market risk can be affected by background risk. Generally, the effect of background risk is to increase the risk aversion of the investor towards marketable risks. This increases the slope of the pricing kernel. However, as we will show, it also changes the shape of the pricing kernel.

Investors may be subject to many different background risks, not just labour income uncertainty, which can affect their demand for risky assets and hence their prices.[16] Examples of other background risks that can affect investors are uncertain bequests, uncertain medical bills, and the returns on non-marketable stocks.

Here, we look at the effect of zero-mean (or pure) background risks by analysing a *derived utility function* for market portfolio wealth. The derived utility is the utility function of an investor who faces a marketed risk in the presence of a second non-hedgeable risk. It has been shown in the literature that the risk aversion of the derived utility function exceeds the risk aversion, in the case where there is no background risk.

So far we have assumed complete markets for cash flows of firms. Now in the case of non-hedgeable background risks, we introduce an element of market incompleteness. However, we continue to assume that the marketable risks of firms are traded in a complete market.[17]

---

[16] Examples of backgound risk in finance go beyond risks that affect individual investors. Franke *et al.* (1998) give several examples. Consider, for example, the case of a multinational company with foreign exchange and interest rate risks which are hedgeable 'market' risks and operational risk which is not hedgeable. Here the operational risks are background risks which affect the demand for foreign exchange and interest rate hedging. Also, consider the case of a fund manager who is judged on his fund's absolute and relative performance. The portfolio risk is hedgeable, but his performance relative to his peers is not. The latter can be treated as a background risk.

[17] The existence of incomplete markets for background risks has the potential for solving at least three major puzzles in finance: the equity premium puzzle (Weil, 1992); the demand for options, which is supposed to be a redundant asset in equilibrium models (Franke *et al.*, 1998); and the herd-like behaviour and seeming underperformance of portfolio managers.

2.3.1   *Consumption Optimisation Under Background Risk*

We now analyse the effect of background risk on the pricing kernel, by looking at the portfolio demand of a representative investor. Background risk refers to a second, non-hedgable, zero-mean, independent risk to which the investor is subject. We show here that an investor with a constant relative risk averse (power) utility function, faced with background risk, acts towards the market risk like an investor without background risk, but with declining relative risk averse utility.

Following Franke *et al.* (1998) consider a representative investor whose wealth at time $t + T$ is given by $w = x_m + e$, where x_m is the aggregate market cash flow, and e is a background risk. Utility is given by

$$u\left(w\right) = u\left(x_m + e\right),$$

where a complete market exists for x_m, and e is a non-hedgeable background risk. In this case, the amount the investor can consume depends not only on the risky payoff, but also on the background risk. The background risk e is independent from x_m. We also assume that $E\left(e\right) = 0$ so that the non-hedgeable income is a pure risk.[18]

The maximisation problem is:

$$\max_{\{x_{m,i}\}} E\left[u\left(x_m + e\right)\right]$$

subject to the same budget constraint used before in Chapter 1, i.e.,

$$\sum_i x_{m,i}q_i = w_t B_{t,t+T}^{-1}.$$

First, we write

$$\mathop{E}_{x_m,e}\left[u\left(x_m + e\right)\right] = \mathop{E}_{x_m}\left\{\mathop{E}_{e}\left[u\left(x_m + e\right)\right]\right\}.$$

---

[18] Gollier and Pratt (1990) provide a good summary of the literature on background risk and its effect on risk taking. The focus of their paper is on adverse (unfair) risks, where $E\left[e\right] \leq 0$. FSS (1998) follow Kimball (1993) and set $E\left[e\right] = 0$.

Then, by analogy with the no background risk case in Chapter 1, the first-order condition is

$$p_i \underset{e}{E}[u'(x_{m,i} + e)] - \lambda q_i = 0, \quad \text{for all } i$$

and, summing over i

$$\underset{x_m}{E} \left\{ \underset{e}{E} [u'(x_{m,i} + e)] \right\} = \lambda.$$

Finally, substituting for λ we have

$$\frac{\underset{e}{E}[u'(x_{m,i} + e)]}{\underset{x_m}{E} \left\{ \underset{e}{E}[u'(x_m + e)] \right\}} = \frac{q_i}{p_i}$$

$$= \phi(x_{m,i}), \quad \text{for all } i. \tag{2.2}$$

Background risk changes the pricing kernel in the following way. As equation (2.2) shows, the numerator is now an expectation of marginal utility, over the background income states. As we will see below, the presence of background risk can have significant effects on the $\phi(x_m)$ function.

2.3.2 *The Precautionary Premium and the Shape of the Pricing Kernel*

In order to analyse the impact of background risk on the pricing kernel, it is useful to introduce the concept of the precautionary premium. Kimball (1990) defines the precautionary premium, $\theta(x_m)$, by the relation:

$$\underset{e}{E}[u'(x_m + e)] \equiv u'[x_m - \theta(x_m)].$$

Hence, $\theta(x_m)$ is the amount of the deduction from x_m that makes the *marginal* utility equal to the conditional expected marginal utility in the presence of the background risk, e. The precautionary premium is analogous to the risk premium, but applies to marginal utility instead of the utility itself.

In the appendix, we prove two results concerning the precautionary premium for the general class of HARA utility functions. We show there that $\theta(x_m) > 0$ when a background risk exists. Also, except in the case of exponential utility, $\theta'(x_m) < 0$. The non-negativity of $\theta(x_m)$ reflects the fact that the risk premium is also non-negative. Intuitively, $\theta'(x_m) < 0$ follows from the fact that a given background risk has less effect at high income level than at low income level. Similarly, we would expect rich individuals to have a smaller precautionary premium than poor individuals. The shape of the precautionary premium for two levels of background risk is illustrated in Fig. 2.4.

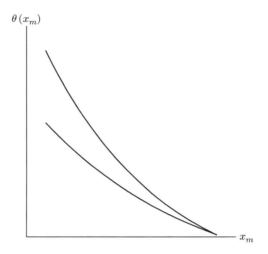

FIG. 2.4. The precautionary premium

Figure 2.4 illustrates the properties of the precautionary premium for two possible levels of background risk. The higher curve reflects a higher level of background risk. For each level, the value of $\theta(x_m)$ is positive and declining in x_m.

We can now analyse the effects of the precautionary premium on the pricing kernel. First, rewriting equation (2.2) using $\theta(x_m)$, we have

$$\frac{u'\left[x_{m,i} - \theta(x_{m,i})\right]}{\underset{x_m}{E}\left\{u'\left[x_m - \theta(x_m)\right]\right\}} = \frac{q_i}{p_i} = \phi(x_{m,i}), \quad \text{for all } i. \tag{2.3}$$

Since θ is positive, the effect of the precautionary premium is to reduce the impact of the constant A on the pricing kernel. Since a positive value of A indicates increasing relative risk aversion, the effect of $\theta(x_m)$, in this case, is to reduce the rate of increase of the derived relative risk aversion. If $A = 0$, the case of CRRA, the effect of $\theta(x_m)$ is to induce declining relative risk aversion in the derived function. If $A < 0$, and u exhibits declining relative risk aversion, the effect of $\theta(x_m)$ is to increase the rate of decline in the derived function.

However, the pricing kernel also reflects the fact that $\theta(x_m)$ declines as x_m increases. This has the effect of increasing the values of $\phi(x_m)$ in the low x_m states relative to the high x_m states.

Background risk has two separate effects on the derived utility of the representative investor and the pricing kernel. First, since the marginal utility of the derived utility function exceeds that of the original function, the aversion to market risks increases. This is reflected in a steeper slope of the pricing kernel. The consequence is that the risk premium increases, compared to the no-background-risk case. This is the effect analysed by Weil (1992). Second, the pricing kernel is more likely to exhibit declining elasticity. This effect will have an impact on the relative value of contingent claims, as we show in Chapter 4.

2.4   Conclusion

In a representative agent economy, the pricing kernel is determined by the relative marginal utility of the agent. In this chapter, we have investigated the properties of utility functions and defined various measures of risk aversion, which are important for asset pricing. We have also defined the prudence of a utility function, which is important for option pricing. Further analysis of the utility foundations of asset pricing are found in Gollier (2000). For a detailed justification of the representative agent economy assumption, see Huang and Litzenberger (1988), chapter 5.

We have emphasised here the impact of non-hedgeable background risks on the prudence of the representative investor and hence on the shape of the pricing kernel. We will see in Chapters 3 and 4, the shape and in particular the decline in the elasticity of the pricing kernel is critical for the pricing of contingent claims.

2.5   Appendix: Properties of the Precautionary Premium

In Section 2.3.2 we showed the effects of a positive, declining precautionary premium, θ, on the pricing kernel. The proofs that θ has these properties in the case of HARA utility functions are shown in Franke *et al.* (1998). Here we summarise the proofs of these properties.

Lemma 1 *With background risk, if $u(x_m)$ is HARA with $-\infty < \gamma < 1$ and θ is two times differentiable, then*

$$\theta > 0,$$

$$\frac{\partial \theta}{\partial x_m} < 0.$$

Proof For the HARA utility function, the marginal utility function u' is a strictly convex function, since $u''' > 0$. It then follows from Jensen's inequality

$$
\begin{aligned}
u'(x_m - \theta) &= E[u'(x_m + e)] \\
&> u'[E(x_m + e)] \\
&= u'(x_m).
\end{aligned}
$$

Hence, $\theta > 0$, since e has zero mean and u' is strictly decreasing in x_m.

To establish the second property, note that for the HARA utility, absolute prudence and absolute risk aversion have the same sign, since

$$p(x_m) = a(x_m)\frac{2 - \gamma}{1 - \gamma}.$$

Also, the derivatives of $p(x_m)$ and $a(x_m)$ with respect to x_m have the same sign. Pratt (1964) established that the risk premium declines with x_m, except in the case of exponential utility. By analogy, the precautionary premium also declines in x_m, except in the case of exponential utility, where it is a constant. ∎

Exercises

2.1. Assume that the utility function of the representative investor is given by

$$u = A - e^{-\alpha w}.$$

Assume that $A = 10$, $\alpha = 0.1$, $w = 1, 2, 3, 4$ each with probability 0.25. Compute the distribution of the pricing kernel.

2.2. Assume that utility of consumption is given by:

$$u(w) = \frac{\gamma}{1 - \gamma} \left(\frac{w}{\gamma}\right)^{1-\gamma}.$$

(a) Compute u', u'', $a(w)$, and $\gamma(w)$.
(b) What do you conclude from these calculations?

2.3. Assume a probability distribution for x as follows:

$$p_1 = \tfrac{1}{3}, \quad x_1 = 10$$
$$p_2 = \tfrac{1}{3}, \quad x_2 = 12$$
$$p_3 = \tfrac{1}{3}, \quad x_3 = 14$$

and an independent distribution for a background risk, e:

$$p_1 = \tfrac{1}{2}, \quad e_1 = +1$$
$$p_2 = \tfrac{1}{2}, \quad e_2 = -1.$$

Assume $u(w) = \ln(w)$, where $w = x + e$
(a) Compute $E_e[u(x + e)]$ for x_1, x_2, and x_3;
(b) Compute λ in the first-order condition;
(c) evaluate the precautionary premium, θ for $x_1 = 10$.

2.4. Let $u(w) = w^{1/2}$. Show that an investor with such a utility function will not pay \$100 to play a game that pays \$150 or \$50 with equal probability.

2.5. Assume that utility is HARA, with

$$u'(w) = \left(\frac{A + w}{1 - \gamma}\right)^{\gamma - 1}.$$

Show that relative risk aversion declines in w when $A < 0$.

2.6. Reproduce the example in Fig. 2.3. Assume that x has a uniform distribution and $u(x)$ is HARA.

3

OPTION PRICING IN A SINGLE-PERIOD MODEL

In this chapter, we use the one-period complete markets model to price European-style options. These options are contingent claims whose payoffs depend upon the terminal cash flow x_j of asset j that occurs at time $t + T$. We show that the value of the option depends upon the shape of the pricing kernel, and in particular on the shape of the asset-specific pricing kernel, $\psi(x_j)$. The analysis starts at a general level and then concentrates on an important special case, where the underlying cash flow is lognormal. We establish in this case that a risk-neutral valuation relationship (RNVR) exists between the option price and the price of the underlying asset if the asset-specific pricing kernel, $\psi(x_j)$, has the property of constant elasticity. This establishes the well known Black–Scholes equation for the value of an option. We also establish sufficient conditions for the asset-specific pricing kernel to exhibit constant elasticity. Throughout the chapter, we derive the *forward* prices of options and relate them to the *forward* price of the underlying asset.

3.1 The General Case

Consider an asset j with a payoff $x_{j,t+T}$ at time $t + T$ and an European-style contingent claim on $x_{j,t+T}$ with a payoff function $g(x_{j,t+T})$. From the complete market assumption, the forward price of the contingent claim $g(x_{j,t+T})$ is

$$
\begin{aligned}
F_{t,t+T}\left[g\left(x_{j,t+T}\right)\right] &= \sum_i q_i g\left(x_{j,t+T,i}\right) \\
&= \sum_i p_i \phi_i g\left(x_{j,t+T,i}\right) \\
&= E\left[g\left(x_{j,t+T}\right)\phi(x_m)\right].
\end{aligned}
\tag{3.1}
$$

Now dropping the time subscripts

$$\begin{aligned} F\left[g\left(x_j\right)\right] &= E\left[g\left(x_j\right)\phi(x_m)\right] \\ &= E\left\{g\left(x_j\right)E\left[\phi(x_m)\mid x_j\right]\right\} \\ &= E\left[g\left(x_j\right)\psi(x_j)\right]. \end{aligned} \tag{3.2}$$

Note that there is an important difference between the expectation operator in equation (3.2) and that in (3.1). In (3.1) the expectation is over all the states of the asset, x_j and those of the market cash flow x_m, but in (3.2) the expectation is only over x_j. We use equation (3.2) in Section 3.3 to evaluate option price assuming lognormality.

As in Chapter 1, equation (3.1) can be expanded using the definition of covariance to give

$$F\left[g\left(x_j\right)\right] = E\left[g\left(x_j\right)\right]E\left[\phi(x_m)\right] + \mathrm{cov}\left[g\left(x_j\right),\phi(x_m)\right].$$

Given that $E\left[\phi(x_m)\right] = 1$, we can write

$$F\left[g\left(x_j\right)\right] = E\left[g\left(x_j\right)\right] + \mathrm{cov}\left[g\left(x_j\right),\phi(x_m)\right]. \tag{3.3}$$

In general, it is difficult to evaluate equation (3.3), given the two functions involved in the covariance term. However, there is a solution in the following example which illustrates the general approach.

3.2 An example: Quadratic Utility and Joint-normal Distribution for x_j and x_m

In this example, we make two strong assumptions that allow us to directly evaluate the contingent claim price. The assumptions are the same as those found in Chapter 1 to be sufficient for the CAPM to hold. However, in the case of the contingent claim here, we need both assumptions to hold simultaneously. We assume both quadratic utility, which gives us a linear pricing kernel, and joint-normality of the cash flow and wealth.

Let $\phi(x_m) = u'(x_m)/E[u'(x_m)] = (A + Bx_m)$ as in the case of quadratic utility, introduced in Chapter 1. Then, from equation (3.3)

$$F\left[g\left(x_j\right)\right] = E\left[g\left(x_j\right)\right] + \mathrm{cov}\left[g\left(x_j\right),(A + Bx_m)\right].$$

Now assume x_j and x_m are joint-normally distributed. Then, we can invoke Stein's lemma (see appendix at the end of the book) and obtain

$$F\left[g\left(x_j\right)\right] = E\left[g\left(x_j\right)\right] + BE\left[g'\left(x_j\right)\right]\operatorname{cov}\left(x_j, x_m\right).$$

Now, assume that the contingent claim is a call option where $g\left(x_j\right) = \max\left(x_j - k, 0\right)$. In this case $g'\left(x_j\right)$ takes the values zero (when the option is out of the money, $x_j < k$) or one (when the option is in the money, $x_j > k$). So $E\left[g'\left(x_j\right)\right] = \operatorname{prob}\left(x_j > k\right)$ and hence

$$F\left[g\left(x_j\right)\right] = E\left[g\left(x_j\right)\right] + B[\operatorname{prob}\left(x_j > k\right)]\operatorname{cov}\left(x_j, x_m\right). \qquad (3.4)$$

The second term on the right-hand side of (3.4) is a covariance weighted by the probability of the option being in the money. If $\operatorname{prob}\left(x_j > k\right) = 1$, then the risk premium is identical to the risk premium on the stock. The forward price of aggregate wealth is

$$F_m = E\left(x_m\right) + B\operatorname{var}\left(x_m\right),$$

which can be solved for the market price of risk, B.

Equation (3.4) has an interesting intuitive interpretation. It says the risk premium for the option is a proportion of the risk premium of the underlying asset. The proportion is the probability that the option will be exercised. Although the pricing relationship is intuitive, the model unfortunately, relies heavily on the use of quadratic utility as well as the normality assumption. Also note that, in order to price the option, we need to know the probability of exercise. In the models below this information is not required.

3.3 Option Valuation When x_j is Lognormal

Returning to the general equation for the value of a contingent claim, (3.2), we see the importance of the asset-specific pricing kernel $\psi(x_j)$ in the valuation of contingent claims. We now assume, more conventionally, that the cash flow $x_j = x_{j,t+T}$ is lognormally distributed. Note that this is the same assumption that is made in the Black and Scholes (1973) model.[19] We now show that a surprisingly simple valuation relationship between the contingent

---

[19] In the Black–Scholes model it is assumed that the price of an asset evolves as a geometric Brownian motion over the period t to $t + T$. This results in a cash flow to the holder of the underlying asset of $x_{j,t+T}$ at time $t + T$ that is lognormal.

claim price and the price of the underlying asset is obtained if the $\psi(x_j)$ has the property of constant elasticity.[20] The valuation of the contingent claim is given by what is often termed a risk-neutral valuation relationship (RNVR) between the price of the claim and the price of the underlying asset. If a RNVR holds then *the relationship between the price of the claim and the price of the underlying asset is the same as it would be under risk neutrality.* The most well-known RNVR is the Black–Scholes formula for the price of a call option. The RNVR is of great practical importance, since it allows options to be priced without knowledge of the risk aversion of investors. We now show that the Black–Scholes RNVR exists when x_j is lognormal and $\psi(x_j)$ has constant elasticity, we proceed, using a sequence of steps.

3.3.1   *Notation for the Lognormal Case*

Suppose a cash flow x_j is lognormal. We now define the mean and variance of $\ln x_j$:

$$E(\ln x_j) = \mu_x,$$

$$\text{var}(\ln x_j) = \sigma_x^2.$$

Using this notation, the probability distribution of $\ln x_j$ is given by

$$f(\ln x_j) = \frac{1}{\sqrt{2\pi}\sigma_x} e^{-\frac{1}{2\sigma_x^2}(\ln x_j - \mu_x)^2}. \tag{3.5}$$

Note that σ_x here is the non-annualised volatility of x_j over a period of length T. It is convenient to work initially with non-annualised variables, since the distance from t to $t + T$ is fixed.

3.3.2   *The Asset-Specific Pricing Kernel*

We now make an important assumption about the pricing kernel. Here we assume that the asset-specific pricing kernel is a power function of x_j:

$$\psi(x_j) = \alpha x_j^{\beta},$$

where $\alpha > 0$ and $\beta < 0$ are constants. First note that if this is the case, the asset-specific pricing kernel has constant elasticity. The

---

[20] Given that x_j is lognormal, the contant elasticity property of the asset-specific pricing kernel means that $\psi(x_j)$ will also be lognormal.

elasticity of the pricing kernel is defined by the relationship:

$$\eta(x_j) = -\frac{\partial \psi(x_j)/\psi(x_j)}{\partial x_j/x_j}$$

and hence in this case

$$\eta(x_j) = -\alpha \beta x_j^{\beta-1} \frac{x_j}{\alpha x_j^{\beta}}$$

$$= -\beta.$$

One consequence of this constant elasticity assumption, together with the fact that x_j is lognormal, is that the asset-specific pricing kernel is lognormal. We have

$$\psi(x_j) = \alpha x_j^{\beta},$$

with $\ln x_j$ normal and hence $\ln \psi(x_j) = \ln \alpha + \beta \ln x_j$, which is also normal. Hence we have

$$\mathrm{var}\,[\ln \psi(x_j)] = \beta^2 \sigma_x^2,$$

and we denote

$$\mathrm{cov}[\ln x_j, \ln \psi(x_j)] = \sigma_{\psi x}$$

$$= \beta \sigma_x^2.$$

Also, for any pricing kernel $\psi(x_j)$, we must have $E[\psi(x_j)] = 1$. It then follows from the lognormal assumption that[21]

$$\alpha = \mathrm{e}^{-\beta \mu_x - \frac{1}{2}\beta^2 \sigma_x^2}. \tag{3.6}$$

We will use this result in the derivation below.

3.3.3   The Risk-adjusted PDF

We now derive the forward price of a contingent claim paying $g(x_j)$. From the complete markets assumption, the forward price, at time t, for delivery at $t + T$ of the claim is

$$F_{t,t+T}[g(x_j)] = E\left[g\left(x_j\right)\psi(x_j)\right]$$

$$= E[g(x_j)\alpha x_j^{\beta}].$$

---

[21] In the appendix at the end of this chapter, we state some of the most important properties of lognormal variables.

To evaluate this expression, we first express the payoff on the contingent claim as a function h of $\ln x_j$. We define the function h by the relation:

$$h(\ln x_j) = g(x_j).$$

As an example, if $g(x_j)$ is the payoff on a call option, with a strike price k, we have

$$g(x_j) = \max(x_j - k, 0)$$

and $h(\ln x_j)$ is given by

$$h(\ln x_j) = \max\left(e^{\ln x_j} - k, 0\right).$$

We can now derive an expression for the value of the claim. The forward price of the contingent claim is given by

$$F\left[g\left(x_j\right)\right] = \int_{-\infty}^{\infty} h(\ln x_j)\psi(x_j)f\left(\ln x_j\right)\mathrm{d}\ln x_j$$

$$= \int_{-\infty}^{\infty} h(\ln x_j)\hat{f}\left(\ln x_j\right)\mathrm{d}\ln x_j,$$

where

$$\hat{f}\left(\ln x_j\right) = \psi(x_j)f\left(\ln x_j\right)$$

is called the *risk-adjusted probability density function* (PDF) for the asset. When expectations are taken under this density, we obtain the forward prices for contingent claims on the asset. We will first analyse the properties of this risk-adjusted PDF and then apply the results to the valuation of the contingent claims.

Substituting the assumed form of the asset-specific pricing kernel, we have

$$\hat{f}\left(\ln x_j\right) = \alpha x_j^{\beta} f\left(\ln x_j\right)$$

$$= \alpha x_j^{\beta} \frac{1}{\sqrt{2\pi}\sigma_x} e^{-\frac{1}{2\sigma_x^2}(\ln x_j - \mu_x)^2}.$$

Now substituting the value for α from equation (3.6) we find

$$\hat{f}\left(\ln x_j\right) = \frac{1}{\sqrt{2\pi}\sigma_x} e^{-\beta\mu_x - \frac{1}{2}\beta^2\sigma_x^2} x_j^{\beta} e^{-\frac{1}{2\sigma_x^2}(\ln x_j - \mu_x)^2}.$$

It then follows from completing the square that (see Exercise 3.2)

$$\hat{f}\left(\ln x_j\right) = \frac{1}{\sqrt{2\pi}\sigma_x}\mathrm{e}^{-\frac{1}{2\sigma_x^2}\left[\ln x_j - \left(\mu_x + \beta\sigma_x^2\right)\right]^2}. \tag{3.7}$$

By comparing (3.5) and (3.7) we note that the risk-adjusted PDF is like the original PDF shifted by the factor $\beta\sigma_x^2$. This is illustrated in Fig. 3.1. Since

$$\psi(x_j) = \frac{\hat{f}\left(\ln x_j\right)}{f\left(\ln x_j\right)},$$

the two curves intersect at $\psi(x_j) = 1$. We now proceed to evaluate this shift factor.

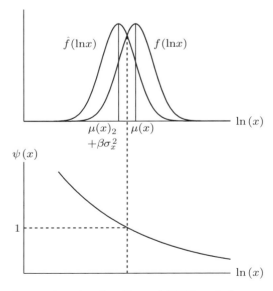

FIG. 3.1. Original and risk-adjusted PDF and the corresponding value of asset-specific pricing kernel

3.3.4   *The Forward Price of the Underlying Asset under Lognormality*

We now analyse the forward price of the underlying asset under the same assumptions. We have, from Chapter 1,

$$F_j = E[x_j \psi(x_j)].$$

Now, since the product of two lognormal variables is lognormal, $x_j \psi(x_j)$ is lognormal, and using result 4 in the appendix (in Section 3.8),

$$F_j = E(x_j) E\left[\psi(x_j)\right] e^{\text{cov}(\ln x_j, \ln \psi)}$$
$$= E(x_j) e^{\beta \sigma_x^2}.$$

In terms of the notation introduced above, the expected value of x_j is given by

$$E(x_j) = e^{\mu_x + \sigma_x^2/2}$$

and hence, in this case:

$$F_j = e^{\mu_x + \sigma_x^2/2 + \beta \sigma_x^2}.$$

It then follows that

$$\mu_x + \sigma_x^2/2 = \ln F_j - \beta \sigma_x^2$$

or

$$\mu_x + \beta \sigma_x^2 = \ln F_j - \sigma_x^2/2. \tag{3.8}$$

3.3.5   *The Lognormal RNVR*

Substituting (3.8) into (3.7), we then have the forward price of the option:

$$F[g(x_j)] = \int_{-\infty}^{\infty} g(x_j) \frac{1}{\sigma_x \sqrt{2\pi}} e^{-\frac{1}{2\sigma_x^2}\left[\ln x_j - (\ln F_j - \frac{1}{2}\sigma_x^2)\right]^2} \, d\ln x_j. \tag{3.9}$$

Note that the expression for the contingent claim value in (3.9) does not include the pricing kernel parameter β or the mean of the asset μ_x. This is an example of what Heston (1993) calls a missing parameters valuation relationship. One parameter of the PDF of the underlying asset (μ_x) and one parameter of the pricing kernel

(β) are missing from the valuation formula. In this case the option can be valued without the knowledge of these two parameters.

However, in this case, the relationship between the forward price of the claim and the forward price of the underlying asset is also a RNVR. A RNVR is a relationship which is compatible with risk neutrality. To see this note that under risk neutrality the contingent claim price would be derived by taking the expectation

$$F[g(x_j)] = E[g(x_j)]$$
$$= \int_{-\infty}^{\infty} h(\ln x_j) \frac{1}{\sigma_x \sqrt{2\pi}} e^{-\frac{1}{2\sigma_x^2}[\ln x_j - \mu_x^*]^2} \, d\ln x_j, \qquad (3.10)$$

where μ_x^* is the mean of the asset under risk neutrality. But, under risk neutrality, the expected value of x_j is also the forward price F_j and

$$F_j = E(x_j) = e^{\mu_x^* + \frac{1}{2}\sigma_x^2} \quad \text{or,} \quad \mu_x^* = \ln F_j - \tfrac{1}{2}\sigma_x^2.$$

Substituting this value of μ_x^* in (3.10) yields exactly the same expression as in (3.9). We see that the claim is priced *as if* the world was risk neutral. For this reason, the relationship between the option price, $F[g(x_j)]$, and the forward price of the underlying asset, F_j, in (3.9) is referred to as a RNVR.

3.4 The Black–Scholes Price of a European Call Option

In this section we apply the general expression for the price of the contingent claim paying $g(x_j)$ to the special case of a call option. A European-style call option, with strike price k has a payoff at time $t + T$:

$$g(x_{j,t+T}) = \max(x_{j,t+T} - k, 0).$$

We now show that the price of this claim is given by the Black–Scholes formula.

To derive the Black–Scholes formula for the value of a call option, we need to evaluate the RNVR in (3.9). The forward price of the option is given by

$$F[g(x_j)] = \int_{-\infty}^{\infty} \max(e^{\ln x_j} - k, 0) \, \hat{f}(\ln x_j) \, d\ln x_j,$$

where the risk-adjusted PDF $\hat{f}(\ln x_j)$ is given by

$$\hat{f}(\ln x_j) = \frac{1}{\sigma_x\sqrt{2\pi}}e^{-\frac{1}{2\sigma_x^2}\left[\ln x_j - (\ln F_j - \frac{1}{2}\sigma_x^2)\right]^2}.$$

First, note that the integral can be written as

$$F\left[g(x_j)\right] = \int_{\ln k}^{\infty} \left(e^{\ln x_j} - k\right)\hat{f}(\ln x_j)\,\mathrm{d}\ln x_j,$$

since the option pays off nothing if $\ln x_j$ is less than $\ln k$, i.e., when $x_j < k$. It is convenient to split the integral into two parts:

$$F\left[g(x_j)\right] = \int_{\ln k}^{\infty} e^{\ln x_j}\hat{f}(\ln x_j)\,\mathrm{d}\ln x_j - k\int_{\ln k}^{\infty}\hat{f}(\ln x_j)\,\mathrm{d}\ln x_j.$$

(3.11)

Now, for the normal distribution, closed form expressions exist for the two integrals required in equation (3.11). We require expessions of the general type

$$\int_a^{\infty} e^y f(y)\,\mathrm{d}y$$

and

$$\int_a^{\infty} f(y)\,\mathrm{d}y.$$

The latter is given by the cumulative density function:

$$\int_a^{\infty} f(y)\,\mathrm{d}y = 1 - N\left(\frac{a - \mu_y}{\sigma_y}\right) = N\left(\frac{\mu_y - a}{\sigma_y}\right).$$

The former expression is less standard but it is shown in the appendix that:

$$\int_a^{\infty} e^y f(y)\,\mathrm{d}y = N\left(\frac{\mu_y - a}{\sigma_y} + \sigma_y\right)e^{\mu_y + \frac{1}{2}\sigma_y^2}.$$

Hence we can evaluate the integrals in equation (3.11) in this case using $y = \ln x_j$ and $a = \ln k$.

Applying the above results and substituting the mean of $\hat{f}(\ln x_j)$, $\mu_x = \ln F_j - \sigma_x^2/2$ and $a = \ln k$, we have

$$N\left(\frac{\mu_y - a}{\sigma_y}\right) = N\left(\frac{\ln F_j - \sigma_x^2/2 - \ln k}{\sigma_x}\right)$$

and

$$N\left(\frac{\mu_y - a}{\sigma_y} + \sigma_y\right) e^{\mu_y + \frac{1}{2}\sigma_y^2} = F_j N\left(\frac{\ln F_j - \sigma_x^2/2 - \ln k + \sigma_x^2}{\sigma_x}\right).$$

Finally, substituting these expressions in the option pricing equation (3.11) yields

$$F\left[g\left(x_j\right)\right] = F_j N\left[\frac{\ln(F_j/k) + \sigma_x^2/2}{\sigma_x}\right] - kN\left[\frac{\ln(F_j/k) - \sigma_x^2/2}{\sigma_x}\right].$$

This is the forward version of the well-known Black–Scholes formula. The forward price of the option is a function of the forward price of the underlying asset, F_j, the (logarithmic) variance, σ_x, and the strike price of the option, k. It is a short step now to derive the spot value of the option. We use the notation $S_t[g(x_j)]$ for the spot price, at time t, of the contingent claim paying $g(x_j)$ at time $t + T$. Since the option is itself a non-dividend paying security, its spot price is given by the discounted value:

$$S_t[g(x_j)] = B_{t,t+T} F_j N\left[\frac{\ln(F_j/k) + \sigma_x^2/2}{\sigma_x}\right]$$

$$- B_{t,t+T} kN\left[\frac{\ln(F_j/k) - \sigma_x^2/2}{\sigma_x}\right]. \tag{3.12}$$

or, using conventional notation:

$$S_t[g(x_j)] = B_{t,t+T}\left[F_j N\left(d_1\right) - kN\left(d_2\right)\right], \tag{3.13}$$

where

$$d_1 = \frac{\ln(F_j/k) + \sigma_x^2/2}{\sigma_x}$$

$$d_2 = d_1 - \sigma_x.$$

3.4.1 Some Applications of the General Black–Scholes Formula

The formula for the price of a call option, in equation (3.13), is referred to as the 'general Black–Scholes' formula because it applies to call options on many different types of asset. To illustrate the point, we apply the equation here to a variety of different assets, including non-dividend paying stocks, and dividend paying stocks.

1. **Non-dividend paying assets**: In this case, spot-forward parity for the underling asset means that the spot price of the asset is

$$S_t = F_j B_{t,t+T},$$

where $B_{t,t+T} = \mathrm{e}^{-rT}$ and where r is the continuously compounded interest rate and T is in years. Also if we define the annualised volatility of the asset by $\sigma_{a,x}^2 = \sigma_x^2/T$ we then have:

$$S_t[g(x_j)] = S_t N(d_1) - k\mathrm{e}^{-rT} N(d_2), \tag{3.14}$$

$$d_1 = \frac{\ln(S_t/k) + rT + \sigma_{a,x}^2 T/2}{\sigma_{a,x}\sqrt{T}}$$

$$d_2 = d_1 - \sigma_{a,x}\sqrt{T}.$$

2. **Assets paying a non-stochastic dividend**: Assume that the underlying asset is a stock or bond, paying a known dividend D_{t+T} at time $t + T$. In this case, spot-forward parity implies

$$S_t = (F_j + D_{t+T})B_{t,t+T},$$

since the forward contract does not receive the dividend. In this case equation (3.13) implies

$$S_t[g(x_j)] = (S_t - D_{t+T}\mathrm{e}^{-rT})N(d_1) - k\mathrm{e}^{-rT} N(d_2), \tag{3.15}$$

where

$$d_1 = \frac{\ln[S_t\mathrm{e}^{rT} - D_{t+T}/k] + \sigma_x^2/2}{\sigma_x}$$

$$d_2 = d_1 - \sigma_x.$$

3. **Assets paying a stochastic proportional dividend**: Suppose that the underlying asset pays a dividend proportional to x_j at time $t + T$. While somewhat unrealistic for options on individual stocks, this assumption is often made when considering options on indices of stocks. Let $D_{t+T} = \delta x_j$, then in this case spot-forward parity implies

$$S_t = F_j(1 + \delta)B_{t,t+T}.$$

It then follows that

$$S_t[g(x_j)] = \left(\frac{S_t}{1+\delta}\right) N(d_1) - k\mathrm{e}^{-rT} N(d_2).\qquad (3.16)$$

where

$$d_1 = \frac{\ln\{S_t/[k(1+\delta)]\} + rT + \sigma_x^2/2}{\sigma_x}$$

$$d_2 = d_1 - \sigma_x.$$

3.5   The Black–Scholes Model and the Elasticity of the Pricing Kernel

In the above derivation of the Black–Scholes formula for the value of a call option, we made two important assumptions. First, we assumed that the payoff on the underlying asset at time $t + T$ was lognormal. We will see in Chapter 4, that different assumptions regarding the probability distribution of the underlying asset lead to different option pricing models. Second, we assumed that the asset-specific pricing kernel, $\psi(x_j)$, has constant elasticity. Again, in Chapter 4 we will explore the effects of relaxing this assumption. However, we first show that, given the lognormality of x_j the assumption of constant elasticity of the asset-specific pricing kernel is a *necessary* as well as a sufficient condition for the Black–Scholes formula to hold. In other words if the pricing kernel does not have the property of contant elasticity, then the Black–Scholes formula does not hold.

The argument follows the proof of Brennan (1979), Theorem 1 and Satchel *et al.* (1997). If

$$F[g(x_j)] = \int g(x_j)\,\psi(x_j) f(\ln x)\,\mathrm{d}\ln x_j = \int g(x_j)\,\hat{f}(\ln x_j)\,\mathrm{d}\ln x_j$$

has to hold for all contingent claims $g(x_j)$ then $\psi(x_j) f(\ln x_j) = \hat{f}(\ln x_j)$, where $f(\ln x_j)$ is the actual distribution with mean parameter μ_x and $\hat{f}(\ln x_j)$ is the risk-neutral distribution, with mean parameter $\ln F_j - \sigma_x^2/2$. From $\psi(x_j) f(\ln x_j) = \hat{f}(\ln x_j)$, we can derive $\psi(x_j) = \hat{f}(x)/f(x)$ which is lognormal (i.e., $\psi = \mathrm{e}^{-\mu_x\beta - \frac{1}{2}\beta^2\sigma_x^2} x_j^\beta$ as before), and it follows that η is constant.

Hence, if x_j is lognormal, the Black–Scholes model (and the RNVR) holds in a single-period economy *only if* the elasticity of the asset-specific pricing kernel, η is a constant (across states), i.e., if η is not a constant then the Black-Scholes model (and the RNVR) does not hold. This necessity result is highly significant because it confirms the crucial importance of the assumption of constant elasticity of the asset-specific pricing kernel. Under the assumption of lognormality of x_j, the Black–Scholes RNVR holds *if and only if* $\psi(x_j)$ has constant elasticity. One interesting corollary of this result is that options on a lognormal market cash flow, x_m, will be priced by Black–Scholes if and only if the representative investor has power utility. This is the result in Brennan (1979).

3.6 Sufficient Conditions for $\psi(x_j)$ to have Constant Elasticity

In this section, we derive one set of sufficient conditions for the asset-specific pricing kernel, $\psi(x_j)$, to exhibit constant elasticity. We assume that x_j and the pricing kernel, $\phi(x_m)$ are joint lognormal. We note in passing that this condition will be fulfilled in a representative investor economy, where the investor has power utility and where the aggregate wealth, x_m, is joint-lognormal with the cash flow x_j. However, there are many other sets of conditions resulting in a lognormal pricing kernel.

As before we denote the terminal payoff on the underlying asset as x_j. We again assume that x_j is lognormal with (logarithmic) mean and variance:

$$E\left[\ln x_j\right] = \mu_x,$$

$$\mathrm{var}[\ln x_j] = \sigma_x^2.$$

We further assume that the pricing kernel $\phi(x_m)$ is also lognormal with (logarithmic) mean and variance:

$$E\left[\ln \phi(x_m)\right] = \mu_\phi,$$

$$\mathrm{var}[\ln \phi(x_m)] = \sigma_\phi^2,$$

$$\mathrm{cov}\left[\ln x_j, \ln \phi(x_m)\right] = \sigma_{\phi x}.$$

If x_j and $\phi(x_m)$ are joint-lognormal, then we can write

$$\ln \phi(x_m) = \alpha + \beta \ln x_j + \varepsilon,$$

where ε is independent of x_j. Then the unconditional expectation and variance of $\ln \phi(x_m)$ are given by

$$E\left[\ln \phi(x_m)\right] \equiv \mu_\phi$$
$$= \alpha + \beta \mu_x,$$

and

$$\text{Var}\left(\ln \phi\right) \equiv \sigma_\phi^2$$
$$= \beta^2 \text{var}\left[\ln x_j\right] + \text{var}(\varepsilon)$$
$$= \beta^2 \sigma_x^2 + \text{var}(\varepsilon),$$

respectively. Then, the conditional expectation of $\ln \phi$ is

$$E\left[\ln \phi(x_m)\,|x_j\right] = \alpha + \beta \ln x_j$$
$$= \mu_\phi - \beta \mu_x + \beta \ln\left(\frac{x}{S}\right),$$

and the conditional variance is

$$\text{Var}\left[\ln \phi(x_m)\,|\,x_j\right] = \text{var}\left(\varepsilon\right)$$
$$= \sigma_\phi^2 - \beta^2 \sigma_x^2.$$

Hence

$$E\left[\phi(x_m)\,|\,x_j\right] = e^{E[\ln \phi(x_m)|x_j] + \frac{1}{2}\text{Var}[\ln \phi(x_m)|x_j]}$$
$$= e^{\mu_\phi - \beta \mu_x + \beta \ln x_j + \frac{1}{2}\left(\sigma_\phi^2 - \beta^2 \sigma_x^2\right)}$$
$$= x_j^\beta e^{-\beta \mu_x - \frac{\beta^2 \sigma_x^2}{2}} e^{\mu_\phi + \frac{\sigma_\phi^2}{2}}$$
$$= x_j^\beta e^{-\beta \mu_x - \frac{\beta^2 \sigma_x^2}{2}}$$

since $E\left[\phi(x_m)\right] = e^{\mu_\phi + \frac{\sigma_\phi^2}{2}} = 1$. Note that x_j^β is a lognormal variable, and the exponential term, $e^{[\,]}$, is a constant. It follows that $\psi(x_j) = E\left[\phi(x_m)\,|\,x_j\right]$, the firm-specific pricing kernel, is also lognormal and has constant elasticity.

3.7   Conclusion

We have established the Black–Scholes formula for the value of a European-style call option, assuming constant elasticity of the asset-specific pricing kernel. The treatment follows a similar logic to that in Huang and Litzenberger (1988). Most other texts prove the Black–Scholes model, using a continuous time model (see e.g. Hull 2003). Cochrane (2001) uses a continuous time process to establish that the pricing kernel has constant elasticity. He then proves the Black–Scholes formula using a similar argument to the one used in this chapter. We will show in the following chapter that the assumption that the stock price follows a lognormal process in continuous time is a sufficient condition for the asset-specific pricing kernel to have constant elasticity. However, the pricing of European-style options is actually a single-period problem, as the treatment here shows.

3.8   Appendix: The Normal Distribution

In the text we assume that a cash flow x is lognormally distributed. If $y = \ln x$ then y has a normal distribution. In this appendix we state a number of results that are obtained when a variable is normally distributed. These are stated without proof. The reader is referred to a statistics text, for example, Mood et al. (1974). If $f(y)$ is normal with μ, σ:

$$f(y) = \frac{1}{\sigma\sqrt{2\pi}} e^{-\frac{1}{2\sigma^2}[y-\mu]^2}.$$

The expectation that $y > a$ is

$$\int_a^\infty f(y)\, dy = N\left(\frac{\mu - a}{\sigma}\right),$$

where $N[\cdot]$ is the standard normal cumulative density distribution function.

We have the following results:

1. The expected value of a lognormal variable:

$$E(e^y) = e^{\mu + \frac{1}{2}\sigma^2}.$$

This follows from the moment generating function of the normal distribution. Also it is a special case of result 2 below. It also follows that

$$E(e^{by}) = e^{b\mu + \frac{1}{2}b^2\sigma^2}.$$

2. The expected value of the truncated lognormal distribution:

$$\int_a^\infty e^y f(y)\, dy = N\left(\frac{\mu - a}{\sigma} + \sigma\right) e^{\mu + \frac{1}{2}\sigma^2}.$$

Following the proof in Rubinstein (1976), p. 422, we have

$$E(e^y) = \int_a^\infty e^y f(y)\, dy$$

$$= \int_a^\infty \frac{1}{\sigma\sqrt{2\pi}} e^{-\frac{1}{2\sigma^2}(y-\mu)^2} e^y\, dy$$

$$= \int_a^\infty \frac{1}{\sigma\sqrt{2\pi}} e^{\mu + \frac{1}{2}\sigma^2} e^{-\frac{1}{2\sigma^2}[y-(\mu+\sigma_y^2)]^2}\, dy$$

and thus the result follows using the definition of the cumulative normal distribution.

3. If $\ln y$ and $\ln x_j$ are bivariate normal, we can write the linear regression:

$$\ln y = \alpha + \beta \ln x_j + \varepsilon,$$

where ε is independent of $\ln x_j$.

4. If $X = e^x$ and $Y = e^y$ are bivariate lognormal variables, then $XY = e^{x+y}$ is also lognormal. Hence

$$E(XY) = e^{E(x+y) + \frac{1}{2}\operatorname{var}(x+y)}$$

$$= e^{E(x+y) + \frac{1}{2}\left(\sigma_x^2 + \sigma_y^2 + \sigma_{xy}\right)}$$

$$= E(X)E(Y)e^{\sigma_{xy}}.$$

Also since

$$E(XY) = E(X)E(Y) + \operatorname{cov}(X, Y),$$

it follows that

$$\operatorname{cov}(X, Y) = E(X)E(Y)\left(e^{\sigma_{xy}} - 1\right).$$

Exercises

3.1. Let $g(x)$ be the payoff function for a call option with strike price k. Show that $E[g'(x)] = \text{prob}(x > k)$, where $\text{prob}(x > k)$ is the probability of the call option being exercised.

3.2. Prove that (cf. equations (3.7) and (3.9))

$$e^{-\beta\mu_x - \frac{1}{2}\beta^2\sigma_x^2} x_j^\beta e^{-\frac{1}{2\sigma_x^2}(\ln x_j - \mu_x)^2} = e^{-\frac{1}{2\sigma_x^2}\left[\ln x_j - (\ln F_j - \frac{1}{2}\sigma_x^2)\right]^2}.$$

3.3. Let

$$\psi(x_j) = \alpha x_j^\beta,$$

where x_j is lognormal with (μ_x, σ_x). Derive an expression for α.

3.4. Explain what are the following: (a) $f(x)$, (b) $\hat{f}(x)$, (c) a RNVR.

3.5. In the following, assume that x is lognormal with $\mu_x = 2.5$, $\sigma_x = 0.3$, $\beta = 0.8$.
    (a) Compute $E(x)$
    (b) Compute $E(x^\beta)$
    (c) Compute $\text{Pr}(\ln x > a)$ where $a = 3.5$
    (d) Compute $E\left(e^{\ln x} \mid \ln x > 3.5\right)$

3.6. Suppose that $\ln x_j$ has the distribution:

p	$\ln x_j$
0.25	1.5
0.5	1.75
0.25	2.39

What is the payoff on a call option with strike price $k = 5$?

4

VALUATION OF CONTINGENT CLAIMS:
EXTENSIONS

In the previous chapter we derived a model of contingent claims prices, where the underlying asset has a lognormal distribution, and the asset-specific pricing kernel has constant elasticity. These assumptions are sufficient to establish the Black–Scholes model for the price of European-style options. In this chapter we extend the analysis in a number of directions. First, we relate the material in Chapter 3 to a more conventional approach where it is assumed that the forward price of the underlying asset follows a given process from time t to the option maturity date, time $t + T$. We show that if the forward price follows a lognormal process, then the asset-specific pricing kernel has constant elasticity and the Black–Scholes RNVR follows. Then we consider alternative sufficient conditions for the firm specific pricing kernel to have the constant elasticity property.

We then extend the analysis to contingent claims on assets with non-lognormal distributions. First, we derive a RNVR for options on assets that have normal distributions, as in the Brennan (1979) model. Brennan shows that such a relationship exists, if the representative investor has exponential utility. We then derive a RNVR for options on assets with generalised lognormal distributions, as in the shifted lognormal case of Rubinstein (1983).

Finally, we consider the pricing of claims where RNVR do not exist. We first discuss Heston's (1993) extension to the case of 'preference-parameter free valuation relationships'. This is a case where at least one preference parameter in the pricing kernel is irrelevant for the pricing of contingent claims. We then derive the related results in Franke, Stapleton, and Subrahmanyam (1999) who showed that if assets are lognormal, but the pricing kernel has declining elasticity, then all options have higher prices than in the Black–Scholes world. Finally, we discuss the bounds on option prices in such economies.

4.1   Sufficient Conditions for Constant Elasticity

In the previous chapter, we saw that the Black–Scholes model holds for contingent claims on a lognormally distributed asset, if and only if the asset-specific pricing kernel, $\psi(x_j)$, has constant elasticity with repect to x_j, the price of the underlying asset. We also saw in the previous chapter that a sufficient condition for this to be the case was that the asset and the pricing kernel, $\phi(x_m)$ were joint-lognormally distributed. In this section, we investigate further sufficient conditions for constant elasticity of $\psi(x_j)$.

4.1.1   *Asset Price Follows a Geometric Brownian Motion*

There is a close connection between assuming that an asset follows a specific process over the period t to $t + T$ and assuming a property of the pricing kernel. This is true both for the individual asset x_j and the asset-specific pricing kernel, $\psi(x_j)$ and for the aggregate cash flow x_m and the pricing kernel, $\phi(x_m)$. In the following, we assume a process for x_m and illustrate its implication for $\phi(x_m)$.

The standard proof of the Black–Scholes RNVR assumes that the asset price follows a geometric Brownian motion in continuous time. Here we assume that the forward price of x_m, $F_{t,t+T}(x_m)$ follows a similar process. First, note that a geometric Brownian motion is the limit of a log-binomial process as the number of binomial stages increases. Now, assume that the forward price, $F_{t,t+T}(x_m)$, follows a log-binomial process with (writing F_t for $F_{t,t+T}(x_m)$)

$$F_{t+1,u} = F_t u, \quad \text{prob} = p,$$

$$F_{t+1,d} = F_t d, \quad \text{prob} = 1 - p.$$

Over any sub-period we must have the state prices q which satisfy:

$$F_t = q F_{t+1,u} + (1 - q) F_{t+1,d},$$

which implies

$$q = \frac{1 - d}{u - d},$$

$$1 - q = \frac{u - 1}{u - d}.$$

The pricing kernel over one sub-period is

$$\phi_u = \frac{q}{p}, \quad \text{prob} = p,$$

$$\phi_d = \frac{1-q}{1-p}, \quad \text{prob} = 1 - p.$$

Over two sub-periods, the pricing kernel is

$$\phi_{uu} = \frac{q^2}{p^2}, \quad \text{prob} = p^2,$$

$$\phi_{ud} = \frac{q(1-q)}{p(1-p)}, \quad \text{prob} = 2p(1-p),$$

$$\phi_{dd} = \frac{(1-q)^2}{(1-p)^2}, \quad \text{prob} = (1-p)^2.$$

Hence $\ln \phi_{uu} = 2\ln(q/p)$ with probability p^2 and so on, which is a log-binomial process. Hence, if $x_{m,t}$ is log-binomial, $\phi(x_m)$ is log-binomial. In the limit, if F_t follows a lognormal process, i.e., a geometric Brownian motion, then $\phi(x_m)$ is lognormal. Hence, a sufficient condition for $\phi(x_m)$ to be lognormal is that the forward price, F_t follows a geometric Brownian motion. Finally, if $\phi(x_m)$ and x_m are lognormal and perfectly correlated, we can write

$$\ln \phi(x_m) = a + b \ln x_m,$$

and hence

$$\phi(x_m) = A x_m^b,$$

i.e., the pricing kernel has constant elasticity.

4.1.2 *Lognormal Wealth and Power Utility*

The result above provides an important link between the option pricing theory presented in Chapter 3, where conditions were assumed to hold for the pricing kernel, and the conventional treatment, where the underlying asset price is assumed to follow a continuous process. Since, assuming that x_j is lognormal, the Black–Scholes RNVR holds if and only if the $\psi(x_j)$ is lognormal, and since from option pricing theory we know that it holds when the asset price follows a geometric Brownian motion, then clearly this latter assumption must imply a lognormal $\psi(x_j)$. Applying a similar argument to the asset-specific pricing kernel, leads to exactly this conclusion.

However, the Black–Scholes RNVR does not require the asset to follow a geometric Brownian motion from t to $t + T$. This is clear from the following alternative sufficient conditions for a lognormal asset-specific pricing kernel. Assume, as in Section 1.6, an equilibrium model, where a representative investor has a utility function $u(x_m)$ for wealth at time $t + T$. Suppose that x_m has a lognormal distribution and $u(x_m)$ is a power function, i.e., the utility function has the constant relative risk averse property. In this case marginal utility is

$$u'(x_m) = \gamma x_m^{\gamma-1}, \tag{4.1}$$

which is lognormal, since x_m is lognormal. Hence, it follows directly that the pricing kernel $\phi(x_m)$ is lognormal. From the results in Chapter 3 we know that this also implies a lognormal asset-specific pricing kernel, $\psi(x_j)$. Hence, if aggregate wealth has a lognormal distribution and $u(x_m) = x_m^{\gamma}$, then the asset-specific pricing kernel, $\psi(x_j)$, is lognormal. Notice here that we have not assumed that the forward price of x_j follows a Brownian motion.

This sufficient condition for the Black–Scholes RNVR is clearly a strong one. Both lognormality of wealth and constant proportional risk aversion (CPRA) were assumed. However, work by Camara (2003) has shown that a much weaker condition is sufficient. Actually, all that is required in this economy is that the marginal utility function of the representative investor is lognormal. To show this, we now assume that a monotonic function of aggregate wealth, $f(x_m)$, is normally distributed and the marginal utility is exponential, i.e., $u'(x_m) = e^{\gamma f(x_m)}$.

From

$$u'(x_m) = e^{\gamma f(x_m)},$$

given that $f(x_m) \sim N(\mu_m, \sigma_m)$, $\ln u'(x_m)$ has a normal distribution $N(\gamma \mu_m, \gamma \sigma_m)$, and

$$E[u'(x_m)] = E\left[e^{\ln u'(x_m)}\right]$$
$$= e^{\gamma \mu_m + \frac{1}{2}\gamma^2 \sigma_m^2}. \tag{4.2}$$

Given that

$$\phi(x_m) = \frac{u'(x_m)}{E[u'(x_m)]},$$

substitute results in (4.1) and (4.2) to obtain

$$\phi(x_m) = e^{\gamma f(x_m) - \gamma \mu_m - \frac{1}{2}\gamma^2 \sigma_m^2}.$$

Since $\ln u'(x_m)$ is normal, this means $u'(x_m)$ and hence $\phi(x_m)$ are lognormal.

Hence, if a monotonic function of aggregate wealth, $f(x_m)$ has a normal distribution, and marginal utility is exponential, $u'(x_m) = e^{\gamma f(x_m)}$, then the pricing kernel has the following expression:

$$\phi(x_m) = e^{\gamma f(x_m) - \gamma \mu_w - \frac{1}{2}\gamma^2 \sigma_m^2}.$$

That is, the pricing kernel is lognormal. It follows then from the result in Section 3.6 that if x_j is lognormal, the asset-specific pricing kernel will have the property of constant elasticity.

For example, with $f(x_m) = x_m$ and x_m is normally distributed, we get a lognormal pricing kernel if marginal utility is exponential. This is the case in Brennan's (1979) model. Alternatively, with $f(x_m) = \ln x_m$, and power utility we get the the Black–Scholes model.

4.2   RNVR on Non-Lognormal Prices

So far, in Chapter 3 and in this chapter, we have concentrated on the case where the underlying asset on which the option is written is lognormally distributed. We now generalise the analysis to assets whose distributions are transformed normal.

4.2.1   *The Transformed Normal Distribution*

An asset price is transformed normal, if a monotonic function, $h(x_j)$ of the price is normal. For example, a lognormal price is transformed normal, where $h(x_j) = \ln x_j$. In this case the function is the logarithmic function. Another example is the case where $h(x_j) = \ln(x_j + a)$ is normal. In this case, a is a threshold level and the price is a shifted lognormal. In this case Camara (2003) has shown that a RNVR can exist. Another important example is where $h(x_j) = x_j$, where the price is normal. In this case Brennan (1979) has shown that a RNVR exists. These are examples, we now consider the general case.

Formally, a random variable y has a transformed normal distribution if $h(y) \sim N(\mu, \sigma)$ and $h(y)$ is a strictly monotonic increasing differentiable function. The PDF of y is:[22]

$$f(y) = \frac{1}{\sigma\sqrt{2\pi}} h'(y) e^{-\frac{1}{2\sigma^2}[h(y)-\mu]^2}. \tag{4.3}$$

4.2.2   The Asset-specific Pricing Kernel

We first establish the asset-specific pricing kernel for the case where the price x_j has a transformed normal distribution. First, recall that $\phi(x_m)$ depends on the marginal utility of a representative investor. We now assume that the pricing kernel $\phi(x_m)$ is lognormal and the asset price has a transformed normal distribution, $h(x_j) \sim N(\mu, \sigma)$. Since $\ln \phi(x_m)$ and $h(x_j)$ are normal variables, the regression

$$\ln \phi(x_m) = \alpha + \beta h(x_j) + \varepsilon,$$

is linear with

$$E[\ln \phi(x_m)] = \alpha + \beta\mu, \quad \mathrm{var}[\ln \phi(x_m)] = \beta^2 \sigma^2 + \mathrm{var}(\varepsilon).$$

Also,

$$\begin{aligned} E[\ln \phi(x_m) \mid x_j] &= \alpha + \beta h(x_j) \\ &= E[\ln \phi(x_m)] - \beta\mu + \beta h(x_j), \end{aligned}$$

and

$$\begin{aligned} \mathrm{var}[\ln \phi(x_m)|x_j] &= \mathrm{var}(\varepsilon) \\ &= \mathrm{var}[\ln \phi(x_m)] - \beta^2 \sigma^2. \end{aligned}$$

Hence, the asset-specific pricing kernel is

$$\begin{aligned} \psi(x_j) &= E[\phi(x_m) \mid x_j] \\ &= e^{E[\ln \phi(x_m)] - \beta\mu + \beta h(x_j) + \frac{1}{2}\{\mathrm{var}[\ln \phi(x_m)] - \beta^2 \sigma^2\}}, \\ &= e^{-\beta\mu + \beta h(x_j) - \frac{1}{2}\beta^2 \sigma^2}, \end{aligned} \tag{4.4}$$

---

[22]   See, for example, Stuart and Ord (1993, pp. 234–242).

since

$$E[\phi(x_m)] = e^{E[\ln \phi(x_m)] + \frac{1}{2}\mathrm{var}[\ln \phi(x_m)]} = 1.$$

4.2.3 The Price of Contingent Claims

We can now proceed to price contingent claims on assets with transformed normal prices. From no-arbitrage, the forward price of a claim paying $g(x)$ at time $t + T$ is

$$F[g(x_j)] = E[g(x_j)\,\psi(x_j)]$$

$$= \int_{-\infty}^{\infty} g(x_j)f(x_j)\psi(x_j)\,\mathrm{d}x_j.$$

Substituting the density function of x_j from (4.3) and the expression for $\psi(x_j)$ from equation (4.4) we have

$$F[g(x_j)] = \int_{-\infty}^{\infty} g(x)\frac{1}{\sigma\sqrt{2\pi}}h'(x_j)e^{-\frac{1}{2\sigma^2}[h(x_j)-\mu]^2}$$

$$\times e^{-b\mu + bh(x_j) - \frac{1}{2}b^2\sigma^2}\,\mathrm{d}x_j$$

and hence, completing the square, this can be written as[23]

$$F[g(x_j)] = \int_{-\infty}^{\infty} g(x_j)\frac{1}{\sigma\sqrt{2\pi}}h'(x_j)\ e^{-\frac{1}{2\sigma^2}[h(x_j)-(\mu+\sigma_{\phi,x})]^2}\,\mathrm{d}x_j.$$

$$(4.5)$$

Equation (4.5) contains the unknown parameters μ and $\sigma_{\phi,x}$. However, as in the lognormal case, these can be solved using a similar equation for the forward price of the underlying asset:

$$F[x_j] = \int_{-\infty}^{\infty} x_j\frac{1}{\sigma\sqrt{2\pi}}h'(x_j)\ e^{-\frac{1}{2\sigma^2}[h(x_j)-(\mu+\sigma_{\phi,x})]^2}\,\mathrm{d}x_j.$$

We now illustrate the general method using the example of a normally distributed cash flow.

4.2.4 Pricing Options on a Normally Distributed Asset Price

Here we assume that the transformation function $h(x_j) = x_j$. This case, where x_j is normal may be useful for pricing options on portfolios of assets, or options on physical quantities, such as corporate

---

[23] See Exercise 4.2.

profits. The example was first derived by Brennan (1979) and was used by Stapleton (1980) to investigate the impact of mergers on debt capacity.[24]

In this case, $h'(x_j) = 1$ and we have from equation (4.5)

$$F[g(x_j)] = \int_{-\infty}^{\infty} g(x_j) \frac{1}{\sigma\sqrt{2\pi}} \, e^{-\frac{1}{2\sigma^2}[x_j-(\mu+\sigma_{\phi,x})]^2} \, \mathrm{d}x_j,$$

where μ is the expectation of x_j and $\sigma_{\phi,x}$ is the covariance of x_j with $\ln\phi$. The forward price of the asset itself is given by

$$F[x_j] = \int_{-\infty}^{\infty} x_j \frac{1}{\sigma\sqrt{2\pi}} \, e^{-\frac{1}{2\sigma^2}[x_j-(\mu+\sigma_{\phi,x})]^2} \, \mathrm{d}x_j. \qquad (4.6)$$

However, from Chapter 1, we know that in this case

$$F[x_j] = \mu_x + \sigma_{\phi,x}$$

and substituting in (4.6) we have

$$F[g(x_j)] = \int_{-\infty}^{\infty} g(x_j) \frac{1}{\sigma\sqrt{2\pi}} e^{-\frac{1}{2\sigma^2}[x_j-F(x_j)]^2} \, \mathrm{d}x_j. \qquad (4.7)$$

This is a RNVR which holds in the case of a normally distributed asset, given that the pricing kernel, $\phi(x_m)$ is lognormal. We now use the RNVR to price a call option on x_j. We apply the following result for a truncated normal distribution, which is proved in the appendix at the end of this chapter:

$$\int_{a}^{\infty} x_j f(x_j) \, \mathrm{d}x_j = \mu N \left[\frac{\mu - a}{\sigma}\right] + \sigma n \left(\frac{a - \mu}{\sigma}\right).$$

Applying this for a call option with strike price k, we have

$$F[g(x_j)] = \int_{k}^{\infty} \max[x_j - k, 0] \frac{1}{\sigma\sqrt{2\pi}} \, e^{-\frac{1}{2\sigma^2}[x_j-(\mu+\sigma_{\phi,x})]^2} \, \mathrm{d}x_j$$

$$= F(x_j) N \left[\frac{F(x_j) - k}{\sigma}\right] + \sigma n \left[\frac{k - F(x_j)}{\sigma}\right].$$

---

[24] Stapleton (1980) models corporate debt as an option on the firm's assets. This analysis of debt using the Brennan model is discussed in Copeland and Weston (1983).

The Brennan (normal distribution) model above and the Black–Scholes (lognormal distribution) model are just two examples of the general result in Camara (2003) for any x_j where the transformation $h(x_j)$ is normal. A further case, mentioned above, is where, for some constant a, $h(x_j) = \ln(x_j + a)$ is normal. This leads to the 'shifted lognormal' or 'displaced diffusion' model of Rubinstein (1983). We leave analysis of this example as an exercise.

4.3 A Generalisation of the RNVR: Missing Parameters in the Option Pricing Function

The idea of the RNVR is central to option pricing theory. However, if the asset-specific pricing kernel does not have constant elasticity, then such relationships will not hold for the pricing of options on lognormally distributed assets. In order to price options when a RNVR does not exist, we might require some alternative method. Heston (1993) generalises the idea of the RNVR in the following direction. He asks the question: when are there missing parameters in the pricing relationship between the option price and the underlying asset price? The idea comes directly from the Black–Scholes RNVR. In the Black–Scholes case, the risk aversion parameter is missing. In this section, we look at Heston's generalisation, and consider whether this can be used to price options where a RNVR does not exist.

Heston considers a class of probability distributions of the general form:

$$f(x_j, \theta) = H(\theta)G(x_j)C(x_j)^{\theta}, \qquad (4.8)$$

where θ is a distribution parameter and H, G, and C are known functions. In order to explain this decomposition of the PDF, we take as an example the case where $f(x_j)$ is lognormal as assumed in Chapter 3. We employ the same notation, with $E(\ln x_j) = \mu_x$, and $\mathrm{var}(\ln x_j) = \sigma_x^2$. In this case,

$$f(x_j) = \frac{1}{x_j \sigma_x \sqrt{2\pi}} e^{-\frac{1}{2\sigma_x^2}[\ln x_j - \mu_x]^2}, \qquad (4.9)$$

which can be written:

$$H(\theta) = \frac{1}{\sigma_x \sqrt{2\pi}} e^{-\frac{\theta \mu_x}{2}},$$

$$G(x_j) = \frac{e^{-(\ln x_j)^2 / 2\sigma_x^2}}{x_j},$$

$$C(x_j) = x_j,$$

$$\theta = \frac{\mu_x}{\sigma_x^2}.$$

However, the class of probability distributions defined by (4.8) is quite broad and as Heston states: 'equation (4.8) leaves considerable flexibility in the specification of the probability density'. Heston, for example, works with examples from the family of gamma distributions.[25]

We now consider asset-specific pricing kernels of the general form:

$$\psi(x_j, \gamma) = A(\gamma) B(x_j) C(x_j)^\gamma, \tag{4.10}$$

where $E[\psi(x_j, \gamma)] = 1$. As an example of the class, let

$$A(\gamma) = a,$$

$$B(x_j) = 1,$$

$$C(x_j) = x_j.$$

Then

$$\psi(x_j, \gamma) = a x_j^\gamma. \tag{4.11}$$

This is the form of the pricing kernel assumed in the proof of the Black–Scholes model in Chapter 3. It has constant elasticity and is consistent with the representative investor having a power utility function. However, (4.10) defines a quite broad set of forward pricing kernels.

We now analyse the risk-adjusted probability distribution function:

$$\hat{f}(x_j) = f(x_j)\psi(x_j). \tag{4.12}$$

If $f(x_j)$ is given by equation (4.8) and the pricing kernel is given by equation (4.10), then the risk-adjusted probability density is

$$\hat{f}(x_j) = A(\gamma) H(\theta) B(x_j) G(x_j) C(x_j)^{(\gamma + \theta)}. \tag{4.13}$$

---

[25] See Heston (1993), p. 937 for a definition and analysis of the gamma distribution.

Equation (4.13) gives rise to what Heston terms a 'missing-parameters' valuation relationship. Option prices depend upon the sum, $\gamma + \theta$, but not on the individual values of the parameters. To see this, first note that

$$A(\gamma)H(\theta) = H(\gamma + \theta).$$

This follows from the fact that

$$\int_0^{+\infty} H(\theta)A(\gamma)B(x_j)G(x_j)C(x_j)^{(\gamma+\theta)}\, dx_j = 1,$$

since the sum of the risk-adjusted probabilities must equal 1. Similarly, we must have

$$\int_0^{+\infty} H(\theta+\gamma)B(x_j)G(x_j)C(x_j)^{(\gamma+\theta)}\, dx_j = 1.$$

Then, the above equation follows.[26] The forward price of the underlying asset is therefore given by

$$F(x_j) = \int_0^{+\infty} x_j H(\theta + \gamma)B(x_j)G(x_j)C(x_j)^{(\gamma+\theta)}\, dx_j. \qquad (4.14)$$

Equation (4.14) can be solved for the sum $\theta + \gamma$ and this can then be used to evaluate the option price:

$$F[g(x_j)] = \int_0^{+\infty} g(x_j)H(\theta + \gamma)B(x_j)G(x_j)C(x_j)^{(\gamma+\theta)}\, dx_j. \qquad (4.15)$$

The resulting option price is a missing-parameters relationship, since neither the distribution parameter, θ, nor the pricing kernel parameter, γ, enter the option pricing relationship. Writing $\theta + \gamma = m[F(x_j)]$ as the solution of equation (4.14), the forward price of the option $F[g(x_j)]$ in (4.15) becomes

$$F[g(x_j)] = \int_0^{+\infty} g(x_j)H(m[F(x_j)])B(x_j)G(x_j)$$
$$\times C(x_j)^{m[F(x_j)]}\, dx_j. \qquad (4.16)$$

---

[26] Note that the two equations imply

$$\int_0^{+\infty} B(x_j)G(x_j)C(x_j)^{(\gamma+\theta)}\, dx = \frac{1}{H(\theta)A(\gamma)} = \frac{1}{H(\theta + \gamma)}.$$

Equation (4.16) is referred to by Heston as a missing-parameters relationship. Notice however, that the option valuation depends upon both $B(x_j)$ and $G(x_j)$. The function $G(x_j)$, which comes from the decomposition of the probability distribution function, we may assume is known. For example, if x_j is log-normal, $G(x_j)$ only requires an estimate of the volatility parameter, σ_x. However, $B(x_j)$ is in general problematic and dependent on unknown additional parameters of the pricing kernel. Unless these can be estimated, equation (4.16) does not provide a solution to the pricing problem. Although Heston's conditions mean that one of the preference parameters is irrelevant for pricing, this is not in general sufficient. This highlights the difference between a RNVR and Heston's generalisation. In the case of the former, $B(x_j) = 1$, and a complete pricing solution exists. In the case of the latter, other parameter estimates are required.[27]

4.4   Contingent Claim Pricing given Non-constant Elasticity of the Pricing Kernel

The conditions for a PPFVR established by Heston (1993) suggests that the occurence of RNVR for the valuation of contingent claims is likely to be rare. For example, suppose we are interested in valuing a call option on a lognormally distributed asset. Then in Heston's treatment the function $k(x)$ is $k(x) = \ln x$, and a RNVR exists only if the asset-specific pricing kernel has the form:

$$\psi(x_j) = ax_j^\gamma.$$

Only in this case can γ be irrelevant for the option valuation. This motivates the current section where we look to price claims in those economies where RNVR do not exist.

Now we generalize to the case where the asset-specific pricing kernel has a quite general form. From here onwards, we write x_j as x. Consider the set of pricing kernels, ψ_h, such that

$$F = E\left[x\psi_h(x)\right] = F^*$$

is a constant. This is the set of all possible pricing kernels that price the underlying asset correctly. Since many possible shapes of pricing kernel are possible under this condition, each pricing kernel could lead to a different option price. Franke, Stapleton,

---

[27] This question is considered in Franke *et al.*(2003).

and Subrahmanyam (1999) (FSS) first show that if the elasticity of the pricing kernels decline monotonically, then there will be two intersections of any two pricing kernels. They then show that if a pricing kernel, ψ_1, has constant elasticity (as in the case of Black and Scholes), and another ψ_2 has declining elasticity, option prices will be higher under ψ_2 than under ψ_1. The results in FSS are shown now in Lemmas 2 and 3.

First, we establish the following lemma regarding possible firm-specific pricing kernels.

Lemma 2 FSS (1999, Lemma 4) *Suppose that ψ_1, $\psi_2 \in \{\psi : E\left(x\psi\right) = F^*\}$, where ψ_1 has constant elasticity, ψ_2 has elasticity that declines monotonically, and both pricing kernels decline monotonically, then ψ_1 and ψ_2 intersect twice.*

The lemma states that if two pricing kernels yield the same forward price for an asset, then they must intersect twice. This is of crucial importance for option pricing, because we are interested in the possible option prices that could exist *given* the forward price of the asset. Different option prices are possible, given the asset forward price, because different shapes of the pricing kernel are possible.

The proof follows by contradiction. First, there must be at least one intersection. If there were no intersection, one pricing kernel lies above the other, implying that $E(\psi_1) \neq E(\psi_2)$, which contradicts the requirement that $E(\psi_h) = 1$ for all h. Second, let there be only one intersection at $x = k$, as in Fig. 4.1. Consider the forward price of x. Under ψ_1, $F = E\left[x\psi_1\right]$, and under ψ_2, $F = E\left[x\psi_2\right]$. By assumption, we must have

$$F = F^* = E\left[x\psi_1\right] = E\left[x\psi_2\right].$$ (4.17)

Now define $x^+ = \max[x - k, 0]$ and $x^- = -\max[x - k, 0]$. Here, x^+ is the payoff on a call option with strike price k, x^- is the payoff on a short put option with strike price k. Hence, $x = k + x^+ + x^-$ The forward price of x under ψ_1 is

$$E\left[x\psi_1\right] = E\left[\left(k + x^+ + x^-\right)\psi_1\right]$$
$$= E\left[k\psi_1\right] + E\left[x^+\psi_1\right] + E\left[x^-\psi_1\right]$$

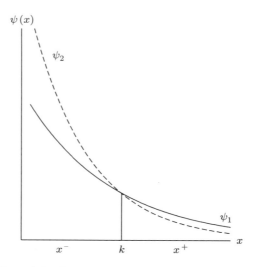

FIG. 4.1. One intersection of pricing kernels

and under ψ_2 it is

$$
\begin{aligned}
E\left[x\psi_2\right] &= E\left[\left(k + x^+ + x^-\right)\psi_2\right] \\
&= E\left[k\psi_2\right] + E\left[x^+\psi_2\right] + E\left[x^-\psi_2\right].
\end{aligned}
$$

The difference between the forward prices is

$$
E\left[x\psi_1\right] - E\left[x\psi_2\right] = E\left[x^+\left(\psi_1 - \psi_2\right)\right] + E\left[x^-\left(\psi_1 - \psi_2\right)\right].
$$

But

$$
E\left[x^+\left(\psi_1 - \psi_2\right)\right] > 0
$$

since $\psi_1 > \psi_2$, for $x > k$ and

$$
E\left[x^-\left(\psi_1 - \psi_2\right)\right] > 0
$$

since $\psi_1 < \psi_2$, for $x < k$, lead to $E(x\psi_1) - E(x\psi_2) > 0$ and the two forward prices cannot be the same. Hence, the case of one intersection contradicts (4.17). Third, if there are no intersections, $E\left[x\psi_1\right] \neq E\left[x\psi_2\right]$, unless $\psi_1 = \psi_2$, for all x, which is the trivial case. Hence the case of no intersections is not possible. Finally, suppose there are three or more intersections, as in Fig. 4.2, then

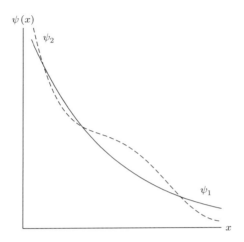

FIG. 4.2. The pricing kernels with multiple intersections

the second derivative of ψ_1 switches sign from $-$, $+$, to $-$, and the elasticity of ψ_1 is not monotonic.
Using this result, FSS then establish that the following lemma.

Lemma 3 FSS (1999, Theorem 1) *Assume that ψ_1 has constant elasticity η_1 and that ψ_2 has declining elasticity η_2, $\partial \eta_2 / \partial x < 0$, where ψ_1 and ψ_2 both yield the same forward price of the risky asset. Then all options have higher prices under ψ_2 than under ψ_1.*

We will prove the result by referring to the case illustrated in Fig. 4.3. In this case, $\psi_2 > \psi_1$ for $x < k_1$ and $x > k_2$ for crossover points k_1 and k_2, and any call option with strike price $k \geq k_2$ has a higher price under ψ_2 than under ψ_1. By put-call parity any put option at $k \geq k_2$ also has a higher price under ψ_2 since the forward price is the same under both pricing kernels. By a similar argument, put and call options with $k \leq k_1$ also have higher prices under ψ_2.
Now consider a call option at k_3, with $k_1 < k_3 < k_2$. In Fig. 4.4, its payoff is ok_3bc. Take a payoff on a linear contract $(-a)\,k_1bd$. This payoff has the same forward price under ψ_1 and ψ_2. The call option payoff is equal to $(-a)\,k_1bd + ok_1a - k_1k_3b + cbd$. The payoffs ok_1a and cbd have higher prices under ψ_2 than under ψ_1 and k_1k_3b is lower under ψ_2. Hence the call option has a higher price under

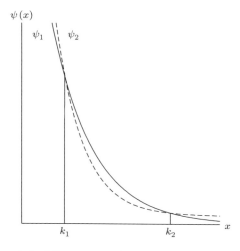

FIG. 4.3. The pricing kernel: two intersections

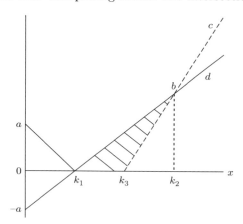

FIG. 4.4. Excess pricing of options

ψ_2. By put-call parity it follows that all put options with strike prices k also have higher prices under ψ_2 than under ψ_1. Hence, all put and call prices are higher under ψ_2 than under ψ_1.

The following important implication is the main result of FSS. If x is lognormal and ψ_2 is the true pricing kernel, Black–Scholes underprices all options on x.

4.4.1 *Bounds on Option Prices*

Assume that x_j is lognormal. If the asset-specific pricing kernel, $\psi(x_j)$, has constant elasticity, we have shown previously that options are priced using the Black–Scholes RNVR. However, if it does not have constant elasticity, option prices may be larger or smaller than Black–Scholes prices.

For practical reasons, we may wish to know: what are the maximum and minimum option prices, given the price of the underlying asset? Or, what are the bounds on option prices? Early work by Merton (1973) discussed rational bounds on option prices, but these bounds are quite wide.[28] Recently, Bernado and Ledoit (2000) have re-visited this issue and their work is closely related to the above analysis given in the work of FSS (1999). Since, from FSS, prices are higher under declining elasticity, then if we could bound the rate of decline (or rate of increase) of elasticity, then we could bound option prices. This is the idea behind the expected gain-loss ratio used by Bernado and Ledoit (2000).

Bernado and Ledoit consider the set of pricing kernels ψ_h, $h = 1, 2, \ldots$ which price the underlying asset correctly, i.e. give the correct asset forward price. They compare these pricing kernels to a benchmark kernel, which could be, for example the constant elasticity pricing kernel, which is consistent with Black–Scholes pricing. They measure the deviation of any pricing kernel from the benchmark by the ratio of the maximum deviation (over all x_j) to the minimum deviation. They then show that the minimum of these ratios over all possible pricing kernels produces the maximum deviation from the Black–Scholes prices. This allows them to compute a bound for option prices. The result follows directly from FSS, since the greater rate of decline in elasticity of the pricing kernel, the greater must be the deviation from the Black–Scholes price. Note, however, in Bernado and Ledoit (2000), the benchmark pricing kernel need not necessarily be the constant elasticity kernel. Hence, the analysis applies more generally than just to the Black–Scholes case.

The main contribution of Bernado and Ledoit (2000) is to show that a restriction on expected gain–loss ratios is equivalent to

---

[28] The Merton upper bound for a call option is the stock price itself, whereas the lower bound is the stock price minus the present value of the exercise price.

a restriction on pricing kernels. The expected gain–loss ratio is defined as follows. Suppose the pricing kernel for asset j is $\psi(x_j)$ and is determined by a representative investor with declining proportional risk aversion (DPRA). Suppose now that an investor has a utility function which exhibits CPRA. There will exist zero-cost portfolios of state-contingent claims that appear 'cheap' to this investor, when priced using his personal CPRA utility function. The expected risk-adjusted gains, divided by the expected risk-adjusted losses from this strategy define the expected gain-loss ratio. The extent of these gains depends on the ratio of the market DPRA pricing kernel to the individual's CPRA pricing function.

The idea behind the use of expected gain–loss ratios is that a cap or maximum on gain–loss ratios is somehow reasonable. For example, if a CPRA investor would not expect to see expected gain–loss ratios above L^*, then this limits the DPRA of the pricing kernels that are possible in the market. This restriction in turn bound the option prices.

4.5 Conclusions

In this chapter, we have considered various conditions that lead to the Black–Scholes model and a number of alternative contingent claim pricing models. We have worked within a single-period model and considered the pricing only of European-style contingent claims. Readers interested in the pricing of options in continuous-time models and the pricing of American-style claims could begin by referring to Hull (2003). A large literature on contingent claims pricing based on continuous-time stochastic processes now exists and a possible starting point for reading is the work of Cox and Rubinstein (1985) and Bjork (2004).

4.6 Appendix

4.6.1 *The Mean of a Truncated Normal Variable*

Suppose that a cash flow x is normally distributed. If x is normal (μ, σ):

$$f(x) = \frac{1}{\sigma\sqrt{2\pi}} e^{-\frac{1}{2\sigma^2}(x-\mu)^2}.$$

Let $N[\cdot]$ be the standard normal cumulative distribution function. This is the probability, under the normal distribution, that $x > a$.

The mean of the truncated distribution is given by:

$$E[x \mid a < x < \infty] = \int_a^\infty x f(x)\, \mathrm{d}x$$

$$= \int_a^\infty x \frac{1}{\sigma\sqrt{2\pi}} e^{-\frac{1}{2\sigma^2}(x-\mu)^2}\, \mathrm{d}x.$$

Applying a change of variables, with $y = (x - \mu)/\sigma$, we have

$$E[x \mid a < x < \infty] = \int_{\frac{a-\mu}{\sigma}}^\infty \sigma y \frac{1}{\sqrt{2\pi}} e^{-\frac{1}{2}y^2}\, \mathrm{d}y + \mu \int_{\frac{a-\mu}{\sigma}}^\infty y \frac{1}{\sqrt{2\pi}} e^{-\frac{1}{2}y^2}\, \mathrm{d}y$$

$$= \frac{\sigma}{\sqrt{2\pi}} \left[-e^{-\frac{1}{2}y^2} \right]_{\frac{a-\mu}{\sigma}}^\infty + \mu N \left(\frac{\mu - a}{\sigma} \right)$$

$$= \sigma n \left(\frac{a - \mu}{\sigma} \right) + \mu N \left(\frac{\mu - a}{\sigma} \right).$$

Exercises

4.1. Assume that w_{t+T} has a shifted lognormal, i.e. $w_{t+T} - k$ is lognormal. Find a utility function such that $\phi(w_{t+T})$ is lognormal.

4.2. Given that
$$\ln \phi(x_m) = a + bx_j + \varepsilon,$$
show that
$$-\frac{1}{2\sigma_x^2}[x - \mu_x]^2 - b\mu_x + bx - \frac{1}{2}b^2\sigma_x^2$$
$$= -\frac{1}{2\sigma_x^2}[x - (\mu_x + \sigma_{\phi,x})]^2$$
and hence establish equation (4.6) by completing the square.

4.3. Rubinstein (1983), Displaced Diffusion Model: Given
$$h(x) = \ln(x - \alpha),$$
where α is a constant and $h(x) \sim N(\mu_x, \sigma_x)$
(a) Prove that
$$\mu_x + \sigma_{\phi x} = \ln(F - \alpha) - \tfrac{1}{2}\sigma_x^2.$$
(b) Use the result to derive the pricing formula for a European-style call option.

4.4. From Fig. 4.3 it is clear that all put options with strike prices $k < k_1$ are worth more under the pricing kernel ψ_2 than under ψ_1. Is it also true that all call options with similar strike prices are worth more under the pricing kernel ψ_2 than under ψ_1 and why?

4.5. Assume that the representative investor has power utility, but is subject to an independent background risk with positive volatility. Show that the price of an at-the-money option on lognormal market wealth is worth more than its Black–Scholes value.

5

MULTI-PERIOD ASSET PRICING

In this chapter, we extend the analysis of asset prices to a multi-period economy. There are two principal differences from the single-period models presented in Chapter 1. First, the asset to be valued produces cash flows at a series of dates indexed by $t + 1, t + 2, \ldots, t + n$. Second, the representative investor has utility for consumption at a series of dates, again indexed by $t + 1, t + 2, \ldots, t + n$. In a single-period economy, all wealth arising at the end of the period has to be consumed. However, in a multi-period economy, an investor has to make consumption decisions in each period. There may be a difference in this case between consumption and wealth.

We consider two distinct approaches to multi-period valuation. The first approach, termed the *time-state preference approach*, treats consumption at different times and in different states as separate assets and derives an equilibrium in a complete market for time-state claims. The second approach derives a period-by-period equilibrium where investors form expectations of the price of securities. This is known as the *rational expectations approach*.

Throughout this chapter we will assume that the risk-free rate of interest is given exogenously. We are therefore valuing assets relative to the value of bonds. We assume that investors can trade in zero-coupon bonds which pay $1 at times $t + 1, t + 2, \ldots, t + n$. However, in the multi-period model, the prices of these bonds at future points in time can be stochastic.

5.1 Basic Setup

1. We assume again that markets are complete and that there is a finite state space. In the multi-period model, this implies that investors can purchase claims that pay $1 if and only if a given state occurs at a given point in time.
2. As an illustrative example, we assume there are just two periods; period t to $t + 1$ and period $t + 1$ to $t + 2$. In this case there are three points in time, labeled t, $t + 1$, and $t + 2$.

3. We wish to value a stock j, which pays dividends $x_{j,t+1}$ at time $t + 1$ and $x_{j,t+2}$ at time $t + 2$.

4. There are $i = 1, 2, \ldots, I$ states at time $t + 1$ and there are $k = 1, 2, \ldots, K$ states at time $t + 2$. The state k that can occur at $t + 2$ depends on the state i which occurs at $t + 1$. For example, we may have a situation where k takes the value 1 and 2 when $i = 1$, whereas $i = 2$ leads to $k = 3$, etc. The general scheme is illustrated below:

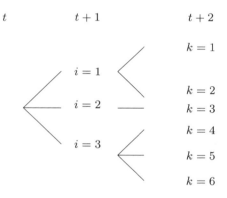

5. Let $\{p_i\}$, $\{p_k\}$ be the sets of unconditional probabilities of state i and state k.

5.2 A Complete Market: The Multi-period Case

In the multi-period case, we assume that investors can buy claims at time t on states at time $t+1$ and $t+2$. In addition, investors can buy claims at time $t + 1$ on states at time $t + 2$. As in Chapter 1, these claims pay out \$1, if and only if the state occurs. This assumption is illustrated in Fig. 5.1. In Fig. 5.1(a), we show the forward prices, q_i, of a claim paying \$1 in state i at time $t + 1$, and the conditional forward price, $q_{i,k}$, at time $t + 1$ in state i of a claim paying \$1 in state k at time $t + 2$. Note that the conditional probabilities for states i and k to occur are p_i and $p_{i,k}$ respectively. In addition, we assume that we know, at time $t+1$, the price of a zero-coupon bond paying \$1 in every possible state at time $t+2$. These prices are denoted $B_{t+1,t+2,i}$. These zero-coupon bond prices are stochastic at time t and are denoted as $\widetilde{B}_{t+1,t+2}$.

In Fig. 5.1(b), we show the forward price, at time t of purchasing a claim paying \$1 in state k at time $t + 2$. Note that

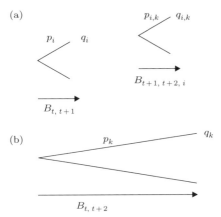

FIG. 5.1. Period-by-period valuation

this forward price, payable at time $t+2$, is denoted q_k. Also, p_k is the unconditional probability of state k.

At this point, it is useful to introduce a notation for the spot price of a state-contingent claim. Let q^* be the spot price of a state-contingent claim. We then have

$$q_i^* = q_i B_{t,t+1},$$

$$q_{i,k}^* = q_{i,k} B_{t+1,t+2,i},$$

$$q_k^* = q_k B_{t,t+2}.$$

These definitions are illustrated in Fig. 5.2.

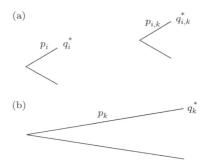

FIG. 5.2. Spot prices of state claims

Now consider the spot price of a state-contingent claim paying $1 if and only if state k occurs at time $t + 2$. It is immediately apparent that

$$q_k^* = q_i^* q_{i,k}^*.$$

This price relationship holds because it is possible in this complete market to buy a claim on state k in two ways. First, the investor can directly buy a claim costing q_k^* at time t. Second, the investor could buy $q_{i,k}^*$ claims on state i and use them to purchase a claim on $1 in state k. The cost of this strategy is $q_i^* q_{i,k}^*$. The equality then follows. Hence, equivalently we can write the following relationship between the forward prices of the claims:

$$q_k B_{t,t+2} = q_i B_{t,t+1} q_{i,k} B_{t+1,t+2,i}. \tag{5.1}$$

The importance of this relationship is that it implies that the valuation of a cash flow x_{t+2} using the unconditional state prices, q_k, must be the same as that which results from a period-by-period valuation using the q_i and the $q_{i,k}$. We illustrate this conclusion in the following section.

5.3　Pricing Multi-period Cash Flows

In this section, we value cash flows arising at time $t + T$; $x_{j,t+T}$. We price the cash flows, first of all using the unconditional state prices. This approach has traditionally been known as the time-state preference approach, as the unconditional state prices reflect investors preferences for consumption in different states at different times. We then show the alternative pricing from the equivalent period-by-period valuation approach. This approach is generally referred to as the rational expectations approach.

5.3.1　*The Time-State Preference Approach*

We proceed along the lines followed in Chapter 1. We start with a case where $T = 1, 2$. First, as illustrated above, q_i is the forward price of $1 paid if and only if state i occurs at $t + 1$. Also q_k is the forward price of $1 paid if and only if state k occurs at $t + 2$. Note that the q_i are forward prices for delivery at time $t + 1$, while the q_k are forward prices for delivery at time $t + 2$.

As in Chapter 1, we have $\sum q_i = 1$ and $\sum q_k = 1$ and also the conditions:

$$q_i > 0 \iff p_i > 0, \quad \text{and} \quad q_k > 0 \iff p_k > 0$$

hold. It follows that $\{q_i\}$, $\{q_k\}$ are each equivalent probability measures to $\{p_i\}$, $\{p_k\}$.[29]

From the complete markets assumption and the Law of One Price, the forward prices of the uncertain cash flows $x_{j,t+1}$, for delivery at $t+1$, and of $x_{j,t+2}$, for delivery at $t+2$, are

$$F_{j,t,t+1} = \sum_i x_{j,t+1,i} q_i,$$

$$F_{j,t,t+2} = \sum_k x_{j,t+2,k} q_k.$$

The value at time t of an asset that pays $x_{j,t+1}$ at $t+1$ and $x_{j,t+2}$ at $t+2$, is then given by, using spot-forward parity,

$$S_{j,t} = F_{j,t,t+1} B_{t,t+1} + F_{j,t,t+2} B_{t,t+2} \tag{5.2}$$

$$= \sum_i x_{j,t+1,i} q_i B_{t,t+1} + \sum_k x_{j,t+2,k} q_k B_{t,t+2}, \tag{5.3}$$

where $B_{t,t+T}$ is the price of a T-maturity zero-coupon bond at time t. As in Chapter 1, the 'forward' pricing kernels in the two-period case may be defined as the probability deflated state forward prices:

$$\phi_{t,t+1,i} = \frac{q_i}{p_i}, \quad \text{and} \quad \phi_{t,t+2,k} = \frac{q_k}{p_k}$$

and in this setup, the forward prices are:

$$F_{j,t,t+1} = E_t\left(\phi_{t,t+1} x_{j,t+1}\right), \quad \text{and} \quad F_{j,t,t+2} = E_t\left(\phi_{t,t+2} x_{j,t+2}\right),$$

and the value of the cash flows is

$$S_{j,t} = B_{t,t+1} E_t\left(\phi_{t,t+1} x_{j,t+1}\right) + B_{t,t+2} E_t\left(\phi_{t,t+2} x_{j,t+2}\right).$$

[29] Hence, the forward price $F_{t,t+T}$ is sometimes written as $E^{Q_T}(x_{t+T})$, where E^{Q_T} symbolises an expectation under the T-period EMM.

The valuation equation (5.3) has an obvious generalisation to the case where there are n periods' cash flows, as follows. Given the zero-coupon bond prices, $B_{t,t+T}$, $T = 1, 2, \ldots, n$, we have the value of an asset with cash flows $x_{j,t+1}, x_{j,t+2}, \ldots, x_{j,t+n}$:

$$S_{j,t} = \sum_{T=1}^{n} F_{j,t,t+T} B_{t,t+T}, \qquad (5.4)$$

where

$$F_{j,t,t+T} = E_t \left(\phi_{t,t+T} x_{j,t+T} \right),$$

or

$$S_{j,t} = B_{t,t+1} E_t \left(\phi_{t,t+1} x_{j,t+1} \right) + B_{t,t+2} E_t \left(\phi_{t,t+2} x_{j,t+2} \right) + \cdots$$
$$+ B_{t,t+T} E_t \left(\phi_{t,t+n} x_{j,t+n} \right). \qquad (5.5)$$

However, as in the single-period case, until we specify further the properties of $\phi_{t,t+T}$, the asset valuation equation is little more than a necessary condition for prices to satisfy in a complete market model.

5.3.2   *The Rational Expectations Model*

We now derive prices using a period-by-period approach, where agent's form expectations of $t + T$ prices, by 'solving the model' for time $t + T$ prices. This is known as the rational expectations approach. As an example of the general case, we first price the cash flow of firm j which arises at time $t + 2$, denoted $x_{j,t+2}$.

We start by pricing the cash flow, $x_{j,t+2}$, at time $t+1$, in state i. From the complete markets assumption, this is given by

$$S_{j,t+1,i} = B_{t+1,t+2,i} \sum_{k} q_{i,k} x_{j,t+2,k}, \qquad (5.6)$$

where the $q_{i,k}$ are the conditional state forward prices. We now define the period-by-period, or conditional, pricing kernel by the relationship

$$\phi_{t+1,t+2,i,k} = \frac{q_{i,k}}{p_{i,k}}.$$

As in the single-period case these are the probability deflated state forward prices. Using this definition we can rewrite equation (5.6):

$$S_{j,t+1,i} = B_{t+1,t+2,i} \sum_k p_{i,k} \phi_{t+1,t+2,i,k} \, x_{j,t+2,k}$$

$$= B_{t+1,t+2,i} \, E_{t+1,i} \left(\phi_{t+1,t+2,i} \, x_{j,t+2} \right), \qquad (5.7)$$

where the notation $E_{t+1,i}$ means the expected value at time $t+1$, in state i.

We now value the cash flow $x_{j,t+2}$ at time t, assuming that investors expectations of the price of the cash flow are given by equation (5.7). We have, again using the complete markets assumption:

$$S_{j,t} = \sum_i B_{t,t+1} q_i S_{j,t+1,i}$$

$$= B_{t,t+1} \sum_i p_i \phi_{t,t+1,i} \left[B_{t+1,t+2,i} \, E_{t+1,i} \left(\phi_{t+1,t+2,i} \, x_{j,t+2} \right) \right]$$

$$= B_{t,t+1} E_t \left[\phi_{t,t+1} \widetilde{B}_{t+1,t+2} \, E_{t+1} \left(\phi_{t+1,t+2} \, x_{j,t+2} \right) \right]. \qquad (5.8)$$

Equation (5.8) says that the value of a cash flow is the discounted expectation at time t of a further discounted expectation taken at time $t+1$. Here again we emphasise the fact that the zero-coupon bond price at time $t+1$ is a stochastic variable.

The analysis now extends in a fairly straightforward manner to the valuation of a cash flow arising at time $t+T$ and then to multiple cash flows. The spot value of $x_{j,t+T}$ is given by:

$$S_{j,t} = B_{t,t+1} E_t \{ \phi_{t,t+1} \widetilde{B}_{t+1,t+2} E_{t+1} [\phi_{t+1,t+2}$$

$$\cdots \widetilde{B}_{t+T-1,t+T} E_{t+T-1} (\phi_{t+T-1,t+T} x_{j,t+T})] \},$$

where $\phi_{\tau,\tau+1}$ is the period-by-period pricing kernel.

Now we find the spot value of a firm j that produces a stream of cash flows

$$\{ x_{j,t+1}, x_{j,t+2}, \dots, x_{j,t+n} \}.$$

We denote the spot value of all the cash flows subsequent to time $t+\tau$ as $S_{j,t+\tau}$. Again for simplicity, we first take the case where $n=2$. First, from equation (5.7), the value of $x_{j,t+2}$ at time $t+1$

is given by

$$S_{j,t+1,i} = B_{t+1,t+2,i} \, E_{t+1,i} \left(\phi_{t+1,t+2,i} \, x_{j,t+2} \right).$$

Now, since investors receive the cash flow, $x_{j,t+1}$, as well as the value of $x_{j,t+2}$, their total payoff at $t+1$ in state i is $S_{j,t+1,i} + x_{j,t+1,i}$. Therefore, valuing this payoff at time t using the pricing kernel $\phi_{t,t+1}$ yields

$$S_{j,t} = B_{t,t+1} E_t [\phi_{t,t+1}(x_{j,t+1} + S_{j,t+1})].$$

Substituting the value of $S_{j,t+1}$ from (5.7), we then have

$$
\begin{aligned}
S_{j,t} = & B_{t,t+1} E_t \left(\phi_{t,t+1} x_{j,t+1} \right) \\
& + B_{t,t+1} E_t \left[\phi_{t,t+1} \widetilde{B}_{t+1,t+2} \, E_{t+1} \left(\phi_{t+1,t+2} \, x_{j,t+2} \right) \right].
\end{aligned}
$$

In general, the value of $T = n$ cash flows is given by

$$
\begin{aligned}
S_{j,t} = & B_{t,t+1} E_t \left(\phi_{t,t+1} x_{j,t+1} \right) \\
& + B_{t,t+1} E_t \left[\phi_{t,t+1} \widetilde{B}_{t+1,t+2} E_{t+1} \left(\phi_{t+1,t+2} \, x_{j,t+2} \right) \right] \\
& + \cdots + B_{t,t+1} E_t \left\{ \phi_{t,t+1} \widetilde{B}_{t+1,t+2} E_{t+1} \left[\phi_{t+1,t+2} \, \widetilde{B}_{t+2,t+3} \right. \right. \\
& \left. \left. \cdots E_{t+T-1} \left(\phi_{t+T-1,t+T} \, x_{j,t+T} \right) \right] \right\}.
\end{aligned}
\tag{5.9}
$$

5.3.3 The Relationship between the Time-State Preference and the Rational Expectations Equilibria Prices

The prices of the cash flows in equation (5.5) from the time-state preference approach and in equation (5.9) from the rational expectations approach are actually the same. The two approaches are just different ways of valuing the cash flows. In equation (5.5), the cash flows are valued using forward prices and long-bond prices. In equation (5.9) the cash flows are valued using the conditional pricing kernels and the stochastic one-period zero-coupon bond prices.

In order to illustrate this, we return to the relationship between the state forward prices in equation (5.1). We have:

$$B_{t,t+2} \, q_k = B_{t,t+1} \, q_i B_{t+1,t+2,i} \, q_{i,k}.$$

This relationship can be re-written in terms of the pricing kernels as follows:

$$B_{t,t+2} \, p_k \, \phi_{t,t+2,k} = B_{t,t+1} \, p_i \, \phi_{t,t+1,i} B_{t+1,t+2,i} \, p_{i,k} \, \phi_{t+1,t+2,i,k}.$$

It then follows that for the single cash flow, $x_{j,t+2}$,

$$\sum B_{t,t+2} p_k \, \phi_{t,t+2,k} x_{j,t+2}$$

$$= B_{t,t+1} \sum p_i \, \phi_{t,t+1,i} \left[B_{t+1,t+2,i} \sum p_{i,k} \, \phi_{t+1,t+2,i,k} x_{j,t+2,k} \right]$$

$$= B_{t,t+1} E_t \left[\phi_{t,t+1} B_{t+1,t+2,i} E_{t+1,i} (\phi_{t+1,t+2,i} x_{j,t+2}) \right],$$

and the left-hand side of the equation can be written as

$$\sum B_{t,t+2} \frac{q_k}{p_k} p_k x_{j,t+2} = B_{t,t+2} E_t (\phi_{t,t+2} x_{j,t+2}).$$

Hence, the values of the cash flow $x_{j,t+2}$ are the same under the two approaches. We will see in the following chapter that the time-state preference approach to valuation is particularly useful when computing forward prices. In contrast, the rational expectations approach is more convenient when computing futures prices.

5.3.4 The Relationship between the Pricing Kernels when Interest Rates are Non-stochastic

We now impose the further restriction that future interest rates are known at time t. The relationship between the pricing kernels in the time-state preference and in the rational expectations approach is particularly simple if interest rates, and hence zero-coupon bond prices, are non-stochastic. As an example, consider the two-period case. As above, the cost of purchasing a claim on a state k is $B_{t,t+2} q_k$. Alternatively, the claim could be secured by first purchasing a claim on a state i at time 1 and then using this to buy a claim on state k. The cost of this strategy is $B_{t,t+1} q_i B_{t+1,t+2} q_{i,k}$. We must then have:

$$B_{t,t+2} q_k = B_{t,t+1} q_i B_{t+1,t+2} q_{i,k}.$$

since both strategies result in the same payoff, i.e., \$1 in state k at time 2. Now, dividing both sides by the probability of state k occuring

$$B_{t,t+2} \frac{q_k}{p_k} = B_{t,t+1} \frac{q_i}{p_i} B_{t+1,t+2} \frac{q_{i,k}}{p_{i,k}},$$

and hence

$$B_{t,t+2}\phi_{t,t+2} = B_{t,t+1}\phi_{t,t+1}B_{t+1,t+2}\phi_{t+1,t+2}.$$

But since in this case, $B_{t,t+2} = B_{t,t+1}B_{t+1,t+2}$, we have

$$\phi_{t,t+2} = \phi_{t,t+1} \; \phi_{t+1,t+2}. \tag{5.10}$$

The forward price of obtaining \$1 in state k is the same as the price paid if two sucessive forward contracts are made. Equation (5.10) will be important when considering values in the two approaches. Generalising (5.10), we have

$$\phi_{t,t+T} = \phi_{t,t+1} \; \phi_{t+1,t+2} \cdots \phi_{t+T-1,t+T}.$$

This equation gives some intuition for the pricing under the two approaches. If interest rates are non-stochastic, the pricing kernel over any long time period, from t to T, is the product of the pricing kernels over the successive short periods from t to $t + 1$, $t + 1$ to $t + 2$ and so on. However, when interest rates are stochastic, this simple product relationship will not hold.

5.4   Multi-Period Valuation Equilibrium: Joint-Normal Cash Flows

In this section, we follow the methodology used in Chapter 1 and evaluate the covariance terms in the valuation equation of the rational expectations approach.[30] We pursue the rational expect-ations rather than the alternative time-state preference approach, because it is possible under this approach to price a series of cash flows, using an extension to the multi-period economy of the single-period CAPM.

To illustrate the valuation, we again consider a two-period example, where there are three dates, t, $t + 1$, and $t + 2$. There is only one cash flow from firm j that arises at time $t + 2$, and is denoted as $x_{j,t+2}$. When we refer to the aggregate cash flow at time $t + 2$ of all the firms we use $x_{m,t+2}$. We assume that the aggregate cash flow of all the firms at time $t + 1$ is $x_{m,t+1}$. We let $S_{j,t+1}$ and $S_{m,t+1}$ be the values at $t + 1$ of the firm j and of the market, respectively. Note that the value $S_{m,t+1}$ includes the cash flow $x_{m,t+1}$ as well as the time $t + 1$ value of $x_{m,t+2}$.

---

[30] The material in this and the following two sections is based on the model developed in Stapleton and Subrahmanyam (1978).

Under the rational expectations approach, the value of the cash flow at time t is

$$S_{j,t} = B_{t,t+1} E_t [\phi_{t,t+1} \widetilde{B}_{t+1,t+2} E_{t+1} (\phi_{t+1,t+2} x_{j,t+2})].$$

Alternatively, this pricing equation can be written as

$$S_{j,t} = B_{t,t+1} E_t (\phi_{t,t+1} S_{j,t+1}),$$

where

$$S_{j,t+1,i} = B_{t+1,t+2,i} E_{t+1,i} (\phi_{t+1,t+2,i} x_{j,t+2}).$$

Note that all the variables in this latter equation are conditional on state i at time $t+1$. Now, using the definition of covariance and the property that $E_{t+1}(\phi_{t+1,t+2}) = 1$, for all i, we have

$$S_{j,t+1,i} = B_{t+1,t+2,i} [E_{t+1,i}(x_{j,t+2}) + \text{cov}_{t+1,i}(\phi_{t+1,t+2,i}, x_{j,t+2})].$$

Following the same logic as in Chapter 1, we now write the period 2 conditional pricing kernel:

$$\phi_{t+1,t+2,i} = \phi_{t+1,t+2,i}(x_{m,t+2}).$$

Now, again following the argument in Chapter 1, if the cash flow $x_{j,t+2}$ and the aggregate market cash flow are joint-normal, then Stein's lemma (see appendix at the end of the book) allows us to write

$$\text{cov}_{t+1,i}(\phi_{t+1,t+2,i}, x_{j,t+2}) = E_{t+1,i} (\phi'_{t+1,t+2,i}) \text{cov}_{t+1,i}(x_{m,t+2}, x_{j,t+2})$$

and defining the market price of risk, $\lambda_{t+1,i} = -E_{t+1,i} (\phi'_{t+1,t+2,i})$ we have the CAPM relationship:

$$S_{j,t+1,i} = B_{t+1,t+2,i} [E_{t+1,i}(x_{j,t+2}) - \lambda_{t+1,i} \text{cov}_{t+1,i}(x_{m,t+2}, x_{j,t+2})].$$
$$(5.11)$$

It is not surprising that the single-period CAPM holds, in equation (5.11) over the second period, since we have in effect assumed a one-period world, with normally distributed cash flows from time $t + 1$ to time $t + 2$. Stein's lemma and the assumption that the pricing kernel is a function of $x_{m,t+2}$ is then sufficient to establish the CAPM.

We now consider the pricing of $x_{j,t+2}$ over the first period. First, it is important to note that the value of the cash flow in state i, $S_{j,t+1,i}$, depends on four variables, each of which could be state dependent. However, given joint-normality of $x_{j,t+2}$ and $x_{m,t+2}$, the covariance term $\text{cov}_{t+1,i}(x_{m,t+2}, x_{j,t+2})$ is non-stochastic.[31] If we assume that $\lambda_{t+1,i}$, the market price of risk, is also non-stochastic, then the risk adjustment term in (5.11) is non-stochastic and since normality of $x_{j,t+2}$ guarantees that $E_{t+1}(x_{t+2})$ is also normal, then the forward price of the cash flow at time $t + 1$ is also normal. However, in order to price the cash flow at time t, using the methods of chapter 1, we require the value $S_{j,t+1}$ to be normally distributed. This will be the case if, in addition, the bond price $B_{t+1,t+2}$ is non-stochastic. In the following derivation we make this additional assumption.

Under the rational expectations approach, the value of the cash flow $x_{j,t+2}$ at time t, is given by

$$S_{j,t} = B_{t,t+1} \left[E_t \left(S_{j,t+1} \right) + \text{cov}_t \left(\phi_{t,t+1}, S_{j,t+1} \right) \right].$$

Given the additional assumptions made above, $S_{j,t+1}$ is normally distributed. Now consider the purchase of claims at t on the value of the cash flow at $t + 1$, $S_{j,t+1}$. We now assume that the pricing kernel $\phi_{t,t+1} = \phi_{t,t+1}(S_{m,t+1})$, where $S_{m,t+1}$ is the value of the market portfolio at time $t + 1$, including cash flows arising at time $t + 1$. The assumptions above are sufficient for the prices $S_{j,t+1}$ and $S_{m,t+1}$ to be joint-normally distributed. It then follows, again from Stein's lemma that

$$\text{cov} \left(\phi_{t,t+1}, S_{j,t+1} \right) = -\lambda_t \text{cov}_t \left(S_{m,t+1}, S_{j,t+1} \right).$$

Hence, a CAPM relationship holds over the first period and the value of the cash flow is given by:

$$S_{j,t} = B_{t,t+1} \left[E_t \left(S_{j,t+1} \right) - \lambda_t \text{cov}_t \left(S_{m,t+1}, S_{j,t+1} \right) \right],$$

where

$$S_{j,t+1,i} = B_{t+1,t+2,i} \left[E_{t+1,i}(x_{j,t+2}) - \lambda_{t+1} \text{cov}_{t+1}(x_{m,t+2} \, x_{j,t+2}) \right].$$

It is interesting to note that the conditions required for the CAPM to hold on a period-by-period basis are much stronger than in the case of the previous time-state preference equilibrium. The assumption that λ_{t+1} is non-stochastic is a very strong assumption. In Sections 5.5 and 5.6 we derive an equilibrium where this condition holds, but the result requires a utility function with CARA,

---

[31] Non-stochastic variances and covariances are a property of joint-normal variables. See for example Mood et al. (1974).

as well as normality of the cash flows. Also, the assumption that interest rates are non-stochastic obviously flies in the face of reality. Various extensions to the CAPM have been suggested to cope with the more general case where the market price of risk or interest rates are stochastic.[32]

Finally, in this section, for completeness we state the general case, where the asset to be priced produces a cash flow, $x_{j,t+n}$, at time $t + n$. Again we assume that bond prices and market prices of risk are non-stochastic. We then have

$$S_{j,t} = B_{t,t+1} \left[E_t \left(S_{j,t+1} \right) - \lambda_t \text{cov}_t \left(S_{j,t+1}, S_{m,t+1} \right) \right], \qquad (5.12)$$

where

$$S_{j,t+1} = B_{t+1,t+2} \left[E_{t+1}(S_{j,t+2}) - \lambda_{t+1} \text{cov}_{t+1}(S_{j,t+2} \ S_{m,t+2}) \right],$$
$$S_{j,t+2} = B_{t+2,t+3} \left[E_{t+2}(S_{j,t+3}) - \lambda_{t+2} \text{cov}_{t+2}(S_{j,t+3} \ S_{m,t+3}) \right],$$
$$\vdots$$
$$S_{j,t+n-1} = B_{t+n-1,t+n} \left[E_{t+n-1}(x_{j,t+n}) \right.$$
$$\left. - \lambda_{t+n-1} \text{cov}_{t+n-1}(x_{j,t+n} \ x_{m,t+n}) \right].$$

5.5 Time-State Preference: Pricing Kernels in a Multi-period Equilibrium

In this section, we derive an equilibrium in which the representative investor's marginal utility function provides an example of the pricing kernels required for the complete markets multi-period model. The model assumes that the investor has a time-separable utility function for consumption in each period.[33] We present a two-period example in which we derive the pricing kernels $\phi_{t,t+1}$ and $\phi_{t,t+2}$ in a time-state preference equilibrium.

Let c_{t+T} be the consumption of the representative agent at time $t + T$. Now we assume time additive utility, where $u(c_{t+1}, c_{t+2}) = u_1(c_{t+1}) + u_2(c_{t+2})$, such that u_2 is not dependent on c_{t+1}.

---

[32] See for example the inter-temporal CAPM of Merton (1973).

[33] This is quite a critical assumption for 'convenience'. It assumes that the utility for different period consumptions are not related.

The agent's problem is to maximise:

$$\max E\left[u\left(c_{t+1}, c_{t+2}\right)\right] = E\left[u_1\left(c_{t+1}\right)\right] + E\left[u_2\left(c_{t+2}\right)\right],$$

$$\text{s.t.} \quad w_t = \sum_i c_{t+1,i} \, q_i B_{t,t+1} + \sum_k c_{t+2,k} \, q_k B_{t,t+2},$$

where w_t is the agent's wealth at time t. We solve the optimisation problem using the Lagrange multiplier method. Form the Lagrangian:

$$
\begin{aligned}
L &= E_t\left[u_1\left(c_{t+1}\right)\right] + E_t\left[u_2\left(c_{t+2}\right)\right] \\
&\quad + \lambda\left(w_t - \sum_i c_{t+1,i}\, q_i B_{t,t+1} - \sum_k c_{t+2,k}\, q_k B_{t,t+2}\right) \\
&= \sum_i p_i u_1\left(c_{t+1,i}\right) + \sum_k p_k u_2\left(c_{t+2,k}\right) \\
&\quad + \lambda\left(w_t - \sum_i c_{t+1,i}\, q_i B_{t,t+1} - \sum_k c_{t+2,k}\, q_k B_{t,t+2}\right).
\end{aligned}
$$

The first-order conditions are:

$$\frac{\partial L}{\partial c_{t+1,i}} = p_i u_1'\left(c_{t+1,i}\right) - \lambda q_i B_{t,t+1} = 0, \quad i = 1,2,\ldots,I, \quad (5.13)$$

$$\frac{\partial L}{\partial c_{t+2,k}} = p_k u_2'\left(c_{t+2,k}\right) - \lambda q_k B_{t,t+2} = 0, \quad k = 1,2,\ldots,K. \tag{5.14}$$

Taking the expectation and adding up over the states, we have

$$E_t\left[u_1'\left(c_{t+1}\right)\right] = \lambda \sum q_i B_{t,t+1} = \lambda B_{t,t+1},$$

since $\sum q_i = 1$. Similarly,

$$E_t\left[u_2'\left(c_{t+2}\right)\right] = \lambda B_{t,t+2}$$

$$\lambda = \frac{E_t\left[u_2'\left(c_{t+2}\right)\right]}{B_{t,t+2}} = \frac{E_t\left[u_1'\left(c_{t+1}\right)\right]}{B_{t,t+1}}.$$

Now, substitute the value for λ into (5.13) and (5.14), and we get

$$q_i = p_i \frac{u_1'\left(c_{t+1,i}\right)}{E_t\left[u_1'\left(c_{t+1}\right)\right]} = p_i \phi_{t,t+1,i}$$

and

$$q_k = p_k \frac{u_2'\left(c_{t+2,k}\right)}{E_t\left[u_2'\left(c_{t+2}\right)\right]} = p_k \phi_{t,t+2,k}.$$

As in the one-period model in Chapter 1, the pricing kernels $\phi_{t,t+1}$ and $\phi_{t,t+2}$ are related here to the marginal utilities of consumption in the two periods. Further, using the Law of One Price and the definition of covariance, the forward prices of cash flows $x_{j,t+1}$ and $x_{j,t+2}$ are given by

$$F_{j,t,t+1} = E_t\left(\phi_{t,t+1} x_{j,t+1}\right) = E_t\left(x_{j,t+1}\right) + \text{cov}_t\left(x_{j,t+1}, \phi_{t,t+1}\right),$$
$$(5.15)$$

$$F_{j,t,t+2} = E_t\left(\phi_{t,t+2} x_{j,t+2}\right) = E_t\left(x_{j,t+2}\right) + \text{cov}_t\left(x_{j,t+2}, \phi_{t,t+2}\right),$$
$$(5.16)$$

given that $E_t\left(\phi_{t,t+1}\right) = E_t\left(\phi_{t,t+2}\right) = 1$. Now, if we substitute the marginal utilities in $\phi_{t,t+1}$, then assume that $(x_{j,t+1}, c_{t+1})$ are joint-normal applying Stein's lemma (see appendix at the end of the book) we find

$$\text{cov}\left(x_{j,t+1}, \phi_{t,t+1}\right) = \text{cov}\left\{x_{j,t+1}, \frac{u_1'\left(c_{t+1}\right)}{E_t\left[u_1'\left(c_{t+1}\right)\right]}\right\}$$

$$= \frac{E_t\left[u_1''\left(c_{t+1}\right)\right]}{E_t\left[u_1'\left(c_{t+1}\right)\right]} \text{cov}\left(x_{j,t+1}, c_{t+1}\right)$$

$$= -\lambda_{t,t+1}\text{cov}\left(x_{j,t+1}, c_{t+1}\right), \qquad (5.17)$$

where $\lambda_{t,t+1}$ is some constant. Similarly, if $(x_{j,t+2}, c_{t+2})$ are joint-normal, again applying Stein's lemma yields

$$\text{cov}\left(x_{j,t+2}, \phi_{t,t+2}\right) = -\lambda_{t,t+2}\text{cov}\left(x_{j,t+2}, c_{t+2}\right). \qquad (5.18)$$

Now, if we substitute (5.17) and (5.18) into the forward price equations, (5.15) and (5.16), and then substitute into the spot price equation (5.2). We have

$$S_{j,t} = B_{t,t+1} \left[E_t \left(x_{j,t+1} \right) + \lambda_{t,t+1} \text{cov}_t \left(x_{j,t+1}, c_{t+1} \right) \right]$$
$$+ B_{t,t+2} \left[E_t \left(x_{j,t+2} \right) + \lambda_{t,t+2} \text{cov} \left(x_{j,t+2}, c_{t+2} \right) \right], \qquad (5.19)$$

where c_{t+1} and c_{t+2} are the consumption levels of the representative agent. Equation (5.19) is a form of CAPM, often referred to as the 'consumption CAPM'. Note that there is no interaction between the first and the second periods in this model. As one can see from the derivation, it is very much like working out the single-period model twice with two separate time periods. Also, the analysis had not as yet solved for the optimal consumption level. Sometimes, the model is closed, somewhat artificially, by assuming that aggregate consumption has to be equal to some exogenous cash flow supply, $x_{m,t+T}$. We now move on to solve a model where consumption levels are derived within the model.

5.6　Marginal Utility of Consumption and Wealth in a Normal Distribution and Exponential Utility Model

In the previous section we priced cash flows within the framework of a multi-period CAPM. However, the price of risk depends there on the marginal utility of consumption in each period. In an important sense, therefore, the model is incomplete, since consumption levels still need to be determined in the multi-period world. In this section we solve for consumption and show that the market price of risk can be re-expressed in terms of the marginal utility of wealth.

Given exponential utility and joint-normality of the cash flows, it turns out that the market price of risk is non-stochastic, as it was assumed in Section 5.4. We also assume non-stochastic interest rates, which once again, as in Section 5.4, leads to the one-period CAPM holding on a period-by-period basis.

We assume a particular form for the utility functions u_1 and u_2, and solve explicitly for consumption, c_{t+1}, as a function of wealth, w_{t+1}. We assume an additive exponential utility function for the representative investor, as shown below:

$$u \left(c_{t+1}, c_{t+2} \right) = -e^{-ac_{t+1}} - \rho e^{-ac_{t+2}}.$$

Here the constant ρ can be interpreted as a discount or impatience factor for delayed consumption. We assume also that the investor can reinvest at a gross risk-free rate R at time $t + 1$, where $R = 1/B_{t+1,t+2}$. We assume also that R is non-stochastic. Then the optimisation problem is one that solves the consume versus save decision at time $t + 1$ such that utility at that point in time is maximized, i.e.,

$$u\left(w_{t+1}\right) = \max_{c_{t+1}} \left[-e^{-ac_{t+1}} - \rho e^{-a(w_{t+1}-c_{t+1})R}\right]. \qquad (5.20)$$

In equation (5.20), the utility of wealth, $u\left(w_{t+1}\right)$, is the (maximum) derived utility of consumption, given the wealth level.

In this optimisation, the investor chooses to consume c_{t+1} and invest $(w_{t+1} - c_{t+1})$. The return on investment is risk free and the investor gets to consume $(w_{t+1} - c_{t+1})R$ at time $t + 2$. The analysis extends fairly easily to the case where reinvestment is in a single, risky asset.[34]

Differentiating (5.20), yields the first-order condition:

$$\frac{\partial u\left(w_{t+1}\right)}{\partial c_{t+1}} = ae^{-ac_{t+1}} - a\rho Re^{-a(w_{t+1}-c_{t+1})R} = 0.$$

Cancelling out a and taking the logarithm of both sides gives

$$-ac_{t+1} = -a\left(w_{t+1} - c_{t+1}\right)R + \ln \rho R$$

$$c_{t+1} = \frac{R}{1+R}w_{t+1} - \frac{\ln \rho R}{a\left(1+R\right)}$$

$$= \frac{R}{1+R}w_{t+1} + k, \qquad (5.21)$$

where k is a constant. Note that R is 1 plus the risk-free rate, so the amount $R/1 + R$ is quite close to $\frac{1}{2}$. So roughly, the investor consumes half of the wealth in year 1. Previously, from the first-order conditions in the time-state preference equilibrium, we found that

$$\phi_{t,t+1} = \frac{u'\left(c_{t+1}\right)}{E\left[u'\left(c_{t+1}\right)\right]}.$$

---

[34] See Exercise 5.3.

Hence, substituting the linear wealth–consumption relationship from (5.21), we have

$$\phi_{t,t+1} = \frac{u'\left(w_{t+1}R/(1+R) + k\right)}{E\left[u'\left(w_{t+1}R/(1+R) + k\right)\right]}.$$

This equation expresses the pricing kernel in terms of the marginal derived utility of wealth.

Now, we assume again that w_{t+1}, $S_{j,t+1}$ and $x_{j,t+1}$ are joint-normally distributed.[35] We can then evaluate the covariance terms. By Stein's lemma,

$$\text{cov}\left[\phi_{t,t+1}, (S_{j,t+1} + x_{j,t+1})\right]$$
$$= \frac{E\left[u''(c_{t+1})\right]}{E\left[u'(c_{t+1})\right]} \left(\frac{R}{1+R}\right) \text{cov}\left[w_{t+1}, (S_{j,t+1} + x_{j,t+1})\right]$$
$$= -\lambda_t \text{cov}_t\left[w_{t+1}, (S_{j,t+1} + x_{j,t+1})\right],$$

where λ_t is a constant. Note that this result is consistent with the general model in Section 5.4. The difference here is that in this model we have a more detailed representation of the market price of risk.

5.7 Conclusions

Multi-period models of asset pricing are inevitably complex. The multiple time periods imply that covariances across cash flows arising at different times are relevant. Also, complications arise due to possibly stochastic market prices of risk and interest rates. In this chapter, we have valued assets using both the time-state preference approach and the rational expectations approach.

The time-state preference approach which leads to the 'consumption CAPM' is dealt with extensively in Huang and Litzenberger (1988) and Cochrane (2001). Pliska (1997) relies exclusively on the rational expectations approach. While these approaches are usually treated as separate models, it is important to recognise that they are just different approaches to the same problem. Given similar assumptions, the two approaches yield the same prices.

---

[35] In fact, we only really need w_{t+1} and the sum of $S_{j,t+1}$ and $x_{j,t+1}$ to be joint-normal. However, it is sufficient to assume that w_{t+1}, $S_{j,t+1}$ and $x_{j,t+1}$ are joint-normal. Also, note that we proved above that $S_{j,t+1}$ is normally distributed.

Exercises

5.1. Assume a state space as follows:

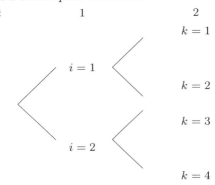

Let the state prices, $q_i^* = q_i B_{t,t+1}$ and $q_k^* = q_k B_{t,t+2}$

$$q_i^* = \begin{bmatrix} q_1^* \\ q_2^* \end{bmatrix} = \begin{bmatrix} 0.4 \\ 0.5 \end{bmatrix}, \quad \text{and}$$

$$q_k^* = \begin{bmatrix} q_1^* \\ q_2^* \\ q_3^* \\ q_4^* \end{bmatrix} = \begin{bmatrix} 0.16 \\ 0.20 \\ 0.20 \\ 0.20 \end{bmatrix}.$$

(a) Compute the bond prices $B_{t,t+1}$ and $B_{t,t+2}$.
(b) Compute the conditional state prices $q_{i,k}$ and the conditional bond prices $B_{1,2,i}$.
(c) If the payoff on an asset at $t = 2$ is given by the vector

$$x_2 = \begin{bmatrix} 10 \\ 9 \\ 8 \\ 7 \end{bmatrix},$$

what is the value of the asset, $S_{t,t+2}$, and what is its (time 2) forward price?
(d) Compute the forward state prices, q_k and re-compute the forward price of the asset, $F_{t,t+2}$.

5.2. If the value of x_1 at time t is given by

$$S_{t,t+1} = B_{t,t+1} E(\phi_{t,t+1} x_1)$$

and the value of x_2, at time t, is

$$S_{t,t+2} = B_{t,t+1}E(\phi_{t,t+1}S_{t+1,t+2}),$$

show that the value of x_1 and x_2 at time t:

$$S_t = S_{t,t+1} + S_{t,t+2} = B_{t,t+1}E[\phi_{t,t+1}(x_1 + S_{t+1,t+2})].$$

5.3. Assume that

$$u(c_1, c_2) = -e^{-ac_1} - \rho e^{-ac_2},$$

and that the representative investor can invest in a single risky asset from $t = 1$ to $t = 2$. Show that

$$c_1 = \frac{w_1 r}{1 + r} + k$$

for some constant, k, and r is the return on the risky asset.

5.4. Explain the difference between the period-by-period pricing kernels $\phi_{t,t+1}$, $\phi_{t+1,t+2}$ and the pricing kernel $\phi_{t,t+2}$. When and why is one or the other type of pricing kernel used in the valuation of cash flows?

6

FORWARD AND FUTURES PRICES OF CONTINGENT CLAIMS

A *forward contract* is an agreement made at a point in time t to purchase or sell an asset at a later date $t + T$. A *futures contract* is similar to a forward contract except that it is marked to market[36] on a daily basis as time progresses from t to $t + T$. This chapter applies the multi-period rational expectations model to analyse the pricing of forward and futures contracts. In particular, we derive an expression for the difference between the forward price and the futures price of an asset. This is then illustrated using an example where the asset price, the pricing kernel and the bond prices are joint lognormal variables. We then consider the futures and forward prices of contingent claims, such as call options. Options are traded on a marked-to-market basis on a number of exchanges, for example, the London Financial Futures Exchange. Futures prices of options can be significantly different from the forward prices of the claims, especially when the options are on interest-rate related assets such as bonds or swaps.[37]

6.1 Forward and Futures Cash Flows

We define futures and forward contracts in the most general terms as follows: A long $(x = 0)$ [short $(x = 1)$] futures contract made at time t, with maturity T, to buy [sell] an asset at a price $H_{t,t+T}$ has a payoff $-1^x[H_{t+\tau,t+T} - H_{t+\tau-1,t+T}]$ at time $t + \tau$. Since for any a, $a^0 = 1$ and $a^1 = a$, $x = 0$ is the case where the long futures receives $H_{t+1,t+T} - H_{t,t+T}$ at time $t + 1$. The case where $x = 1$ is

---

[36] If a contract is marked to market, gains and losses due to daily price changes are settled immediately, usually through a margin account.

[37] A classic article distinguishing the behaviour and pricing of forward and futures contracts is Cox, Ingersoll, and Ross (1981) (CIR). CIR characterised the payoff on futures and forward contracts, allowing us to price these contracts using the multi-period methods of Chapter 5. This chapter also relies heavily on the paper by Satchell *et al.* (1997) which applied many of the ideas in CIR to price futures and forwards on contingent claims.

the case where the short futures receives $-H_{t+1,t+T} + H_{t,t+T}$ at time $t+1$. The payoff on a forward contract is $-1^x[S_{t+T} - F_{t,t+T}]$ at time $t+T$, thus $x = 0$ is the case where the long forward receives $S_{t+T} - F_{t,t+T}$ at time $t+T$. The case where $x = 1$ is the case where the short forward receives $-S_{t+T} + F_{t,t+T}$ at time $t + T$.

The payoff on the futures contract at $t + T$ depends on the difference between the futures price on that day and the price on the previous day. The cash flow profile for a long futures is shown in the first half of the following table. The payoff on a long forward contract at a price $F_{t,t+T}$ is shown in the second part of the table.

	$t+1$	$t+2$	$t+3$	$\cdots$	$t+T$
Futures	$H_{t+1,t+T}$	$H_{t+2,t+T}$	$H_{t+3,t+T}$	$\cdots$	$H_{t+T,t+T}$
contract	$-H_{t,t+T}$	$-H_{t+1,t+T}$	$-H_{t+2,t+T}$	$\cdots$	$-H_{t+T-1,t+T}$
Forward					S_{t+T}
contract					$-F_{t,t+T}$

Since the futures price $H_{t+T,t+T}$ must converge to S_{t+T} as $t+T$ approaches, it follows that the sum of the cash flows accruing to the futures contract equals the payoff on a forward contract if $F_{t,t+T} = H_{t,t+T}$.

6.2   No-arbitrage Relationships

Cox *et al.* (1981) characterised the payoff on futures and forward contracts. First, they established the following lemma:

Lemma 4 (CIR (1981) Proposition 1) *Consider an asset with a price $\widetilde{S}_{t+T}$ at time $t + T$. The futures price of the asset, $H_{t,t+T}$, is the time t spot price of an asset which has a payoff*

$$\frac{\widetilde{S}_{t+T}}{B_{t,t+1}\widetilde{B}_{t+1,t+2}\cdots\widetilde{B}_{t+T-1,t+T}}$$

at time $t + T$.

Note that here, we have used the notation $\widetilde{S}$ and $\widetilde{B}$, in order to emphasize the fact that the future asset price and zero-coupon bond prices are stochastic.

The importance of this result stems from the fact that it turns the futures price into the price of a physical asset that could exist. This asset can be valued using the formulae derived in the previous chapter. We first give a simple proof of the lemma. We will then use it, together with the rational expectations method, to find the futures price.

Proof We start with $1/B_{t,t+1}$ long futures contracts at time t. The futures position on day τ is increased by multiplying the previous position by $1/B_{t+\tau,\tau+1}$. We consider a three-period case, where $t = 0$ and the futures matures at $T = 3$. Hence the strategy is to take $1/B_{0,1}$ long futures at $t = 0$, $1/(B_{0,1}B_{1,2})$ long futures at $\tau = 1$, and $1/(B_{0,1}B_{1,2}B_{2,3})$ long futures at $\tau = 2$. Invest all gains/losses from the futures positions overnight and earn/pay the overnight rate $1/B_{t+\tau,\tau+1}$ on these. Also, at time $t = 0$, invest an amount $H_{0,3}$ in a one-period risk-free bond and roll it over at each period at the one-period rate.

The period-by-period cash flows resulting from this strategy are as shown in the following table:

Time	Profits from futures	Gain from investment	Net position
0	—	—	$H_{0,3}$
1	$\frac{1}{B_{0,1}}[H_{1,3} - H_{0,3}]$	$\frac{1}{B_{0,1}}[H_{0,3}]$	$\frac{1}{B_{0,1}}[H_{1,3}]$
2	$\frac{1}{B_{0,1}B_{1,2}}[H_{2,3} - H_{1,3}]$	$\frac{1}{B_{0,1}B_{1,2}}[H_{1,3}]$	$\frac{1}{B_{0,1}B_{1,2}}[H_{2,3}]$
3	$\frac{1}{B_{0,1}B_{1,2}B_{2,3}}[H_{3,3} - H_{2,3}]$	$\frac{1}{B_{0,1}B_{1,2}B_{2,3}}[H_{2,3}]$	$\frac{1}{B_{0,1}B_{1,2}B_{2,3}}[H_{3,3}]$

Since the futures price for immediate delivery at $t = 3$ is $H_{3,3} = S_3$, the strategy turns an investment of $H_{0,3}$ into a cash flow of $S_3/(B_{0,1}B_{1,2}B_{2,3})$. In general, an investment of $H_{t,t+T}$ at time t can be turned into $\widetilde{S}_{t+T}/(B_{t,t+1}B_{t+1,t+2}B_{t+2,t+3} \cdots B_{t+T-1,t+T})$ at time $t+T$. Hence $H_{t,t+T}$ must be the spot price of this payoff. ∎

A very similar argument can be used to characterise the forward price of an asset. We have the following lemma:

Lemma 5 (CIR Proposition 2) *Consider an asset with a price $\widetilde{S}_{t+T}$ at time $t + T$. The forward price of the asset, $F_{t,t+T}$, is the* *time t spot price of an asset which has a payoff*

$$\frac{\widetilde{S}_{t+T}}{B_{t,t+T}}$$

at time t + T.

Proof To prove this proposition, consider the following strategy. Invest $F_{t,t+T}$ in a T-maturity risk-free bond at time t at the long bond price, $B_{t,t+T}$. At the same time, take out $1/B_{t,t+T}$ long forward contracts to buy the asset. At time $t + T$, the payoff of the risk-free bond investment is $F_{t,t+T}/B_{t,t+T}$, and the payoff from the forward contract is $\widetilde{S}_{t+T} - F_{t,t+T}/B_{t,t+T}$. At time $t + T$, the combined position is $\widetilde{S}_{t+T}/B_{t,t+T}$. So $F_{t,t+T}$ is the time t value of $\widetilde{S}_{t+T}/B_{t,t+T}$. ∎

Lemmas 4 and 5 allow us to find the futures price $H_{t,t+T}$ and the forward price $F_{t,t+T}$ by valuing the payoffs of the assets in the lemmas.

6.3 Forward and Futures Prices in a Rational Expectations Model

In this section, we use the rational expectations framework to derive the futures price of an asset, using the CIR (1981) Proposition 1. From the analysis in Chapter 5, the spot price, S_t, of a period $t + 3$ cash flow, x_{t+3}, is given by

$$S_t = B_{t,t+1} E_t \{\phi_{t,t+1} B_{t+1,t+2} E_{t+1} [\phi_{t+1,t+2} B_{t+2,t+3}$$
$$E_{t+2} (\phi_{t+2,t+3} \ x_{t+3})]\},$$

where $\phi_{\tau,\tau+1}$, are the period-by-period pricing kernels. Since the bond price, $B_{t,t+1}$, is known at time t, and $B_{t+1,t+2}$, is known at time $t + 1$, and so on, we can write S_t as

$$S_t = E_t \{\phi_{t,t+1} E_{t+1} [\phi_{t+1,t+2}$$
$$E_{t+2} (\phi_{t+2,t+3} \ B_{t,t+1} B_{t+1,t+2} B_{t+2,t+3} x_{t+3})]\},$$

In general, we can write

$$S_t = E_t \left\{ \phi_{t,t+1} E_{t+1} \left[\phi_{t+1,t+2} \cdots \right.\right.$$

$$\left.\left. E_{t+T-1} \left(\phi_{t+T-1,t+T} \prod_{\tau=1}^{T} B_{t+\tau-1,t+\tau} x_{t+T} \right) \right] \right\}. \quad (6.1)$$

In order to simplify the notation, we now write $E_t^Q(S_{t+1}) = E_t(S_{t+1}\phi_{t,t+1})$, for all t. Here E_t^Q is often referred to as the expectation under the 'risk-neutral' measure.[38] Using this convention, the price of the cash flow, x_{t+3}, can be written as:

$$S_t = E_t^Q \left\{ E_{t+1}^Q \left[E_{t+2}^Q \left(B_{t,t+1} B_{t+1,t+2} B_{t+2,t+3} x_{t+3} \right) \right] \right\}$$

$$= E_t^Q \left(B_{t,t+1} B_{t+1,t+2} B_{t+2,t+3} x_{t+3} \right). \quad (6.2)$$

This last step follows from the 'tower' property of expectations. Hence, under the rational expectations approach, the price of a cash flow is the expected value, under the risk-neutral measure, of the discounted cash flow, where the discount rate is the product of the period-by-period bond prices. In general, the cash flow arising at time $t + T$, has a price

$$S_t = E_t^Q \left(\prod_{\tau=1}^{T} B_{t+\tau-1,t+\tau} x_{t+T} \right). \quad (6.3)$$

We can now find the futures price by applying CIR Proposition 1 and equation (6.3). From CIR Proposition 1, the futures price of a cash flow x_{t+3} is the spot price of an asset paying

$$\frac{x_{t+3}}{B_{t,t+1} B_{t+1,t+2} B_{t+2,t+3}},$$

---

[38] To be precise, $E_t^Q(\cdot)$ is the expectation under the period-by-period risk-neutral measure. Some writers retain the use of the term risk-neutral measure for the case where the period from t to $t+1$ is very short, i.e., the continuous case. Note that

$$E_t^Q[E_{t+1}^Q(S_{t+2})] = E_t[\phi_{t,t+1} E_{t+1}(\phi_{t+1,t+2} S_{t+2})].$$

at time $t + 3$. Substituting this payoff in equation (6.2), we have

$$H_{t,t+3} = E_t^Q(x_{t+3}),$$

since all the discount factors cancel out. The futures price is simply the expectation, under the risk-neutral measure of the cash flow x_{t+3}. In general, we have the following important result:

$$H_{t,t+T} = E_t^Q(x_{t+T}). \tag{6.4}$$

The fact that the futures price is the expected value of the cash flow, under the risk-neutral measure, has a number of interesting implications. First, if we define *local risk-neutrality* as the case where $\phi_{t,t+1} = 1$, for all t, then $H_{t,t+T} = E_t(x_{t+T})$. The futures price is the expected spot price under local risk neutrality.[39] Second, the futures price follows a martingale, under the risk-neutral measure. To see this note that $H_{t+1,t+T} = E_{t+1}^Q(x_{t+T})$ and the time t futures price is

$$H_{t,t+T} = E_t^Q(x_{t+T})$$
$$= E_t^Q\left[E_{t+1}^Q(x_{t+T})\right]$$
$$= E_t^Q(H_{t+1,t+T}).$$

At any date, t, the futures price is the expected value, under the risk-neutral measure, of the subsequent futures price. Third, consider now the futures price of a European-style contingent claim, paying $g(x_{t+T})$ at time $t + T$. This is the price that would be agreed, if the claim was traded on a marked-to-market basis. We denote this futures price as $H_{t,t+T}[g(x_{t+T})]$. Then, using (6.4), we have

$$H_{t,t+T}[g(x_{t+T})] = E_t^Q[g(x_{t+T})].$$

This relationship will be used later to find the futures price of an option, under more specific assumptions.

We now consider the forward price of a cash flow. Again we take the example where $T = 3$. Using Lemma 5, the forward price of $x_{t,t+3}$ is the spot price of an asset paying $x_{t,t+3}/B_{t,t+3}$ at time

---

[39] It is worth noting, that $\phi_{t,t+1} = 1$ is a sufficient, but not a necessary condition for $H_{t,t+T} = E_t(x_{t+T})$. If the asset specific pricing kernel $\psi_{t,t+1} = 1$, this is sufficient.

$t+3$. Again using the rational expectations valuation equation, we have the forward price

$$F_{t,t+T} = E_t^Q \left(\frac{B_{t,t+1}B_{t+1,t+2}B_{t+2,t+3}x_{t+3}}{B_{t,t+3}} \right).$$

In general, the forward price of the cash flow arising at time $t+T$, is

$$F_{t,t+T} = E_t^Q \left(\prod_{\tau=1}^{T} \frac{B_{t+\tau-1,t+\tau}}{B_{t,t+T}} x_{t+T} \right).$$

The first thing to note is the complexity of the forward price, in comparison to the futures price. The forward price involves all the future, stochastic bond prices, that cannot be cancelled out as they are in deriving the futures pricing formula. The forward price is not, in general, equal to the expected value of the cash flow under the period-by-period risk-neutral measure. Neither is it a martingale under this probability measure. Now define a new variable:

$$b_{t,t+T} = \prod_{\tau=1}^{T} \frac{B_{t+\tau-1,t+\tau}}{B_{t,t+T}},$$

where $b_{t,t+T}$ is the inverse of the amount obtained by borrowing $B_{t,t+T}$ long-term and investing it in an overnight account throughout the period from t to $t + T$. Using this definition, the forward price is

$$F_{t,t+T} = E_t^Q(b_{t,t+T}x_{t+T}). \tag{6.5}$$

It follows from (6.5), by setting $x_{t+T} = 1$ that

$$E_t^Q(b_{t,t+T}) = 1.$$

We can now evaluate the forward price and compare it with the futures price. Expanding the expected product term in the forward price equation yields[40]

$$F_{t,t+T} = E_t^Q(b_{t,t+T})E_t^Q(x_{t+T}) + \text{cov}^Q(b_{t,t+T}, x_{t+T}).$$

---

[40] In order to understand the meaning of the cov^Q term it is necessary to step back to the original definition of the expectation E^Q.

Since the first term equals 1 and the second term is the futures price, we have

$$F_{t,t+T} = H_{t,t+T} + \text{cov}^Q(b_{t,t+T}, x_{t+T}). \qquad (6.6)$$

Clearly, the forward price of a cash flow will exceed the futures price if the covariance term in (6.6) is positive. There is some reason to believe that for some assets, the covariance between x_{t+T} and $b_{t,t+T}$ is positive, this is because if $b_{t,t+T}$ is negatively related to interest rates and the payoff on cash flows from stocks or bonds may also be negatively related to interest rates. However, the covariance in (6.6) is a covariance, under the risk-neutral measure. In order to evaluate this covariance, we will make more specific assumptions in the following section.[41]

6.4   Futures and Forward Prices given Lognormal Variables

Explicit formulae relating the futures, forward and the spot prices of an asset are somewhat rare. It is useful therefore to consider special cases where the distribution of the asset payoff, the pricing kernel, and the stochastic future bond prices are specified. In this section we assume, as in Chapter 3 that the cash payoff, x_{t+T} has a lognormal distribution. Also, the pricing kernel $\phi_{\tau,\tau+1}$ and the zero-coupon bond price are assumed to be lognormal over each future time period.

If the bond price $B_{\tau,\tau+1}$ is lognormal, then this implies that $b_{t,t+T}$ is also lognormal, since $b_{t,t+T}$ is the product of future bond prices.[42] We now define a new variable by the relationship

$$\phi^*_{t,t+T} = \prod_{\tau=1}^{T} \phi_{t+\tau-1,t+\tau}. \qquad (6.7)$$

It follows that if $\phi_{\tau,\tau+1}$ is lognormal, the product term, $\phi^*_{t,t+T}$, in (6.7) is also lognormal. Using this definition, equation (6.1) for the

---

[41] A similar relationship to that in (6.6) was first derived in Cox *et al.* (1985*a,b*) assuming geometric Brownian motion.

[42] Since the sum of a set of normal variables is itself normal, then the product of a set of lognormal variables must be lognormal.

spot price can be written as[43]

$$S_{t,t+T} = E_t \left(\phi^*_{t,t+T} b_{t,t+T} B_{t,t+T} x_{t+T} \right).$$

The corresponding expressions for the futures price and the forward price, using this notation are:

$$H_{t,t+T} = E_t \left(\phi^*_{t,t+T} x_{t+T} \right).$$
$$F_{t,t+T} = E_t \left(\phi^*_{t,t+T} b_{t,t+T} x_{t+T} \right).$$

In order to obtain explicit formulae for the futures and the forward price of the cash flow under lognormality, we follow the logic of Chapter 3.

First, the futures price from (6.4) is

$$H_{t,t+T} = E \left(x_{t+T} \phi^*_{t,t+T} \right).$$

Now, substitute $\mu_x = E \left(\ln x_{t+T} \right)$ and $\mu_\phi = E \left(\ln \phi^*_{t,T} \right)$ and take logarithms to yield

$$\ln E \left(x_{t+T} \phi^*_{t,t+T} \right) = \mu_x + \mu_\phi + \frac{1}{2} \left(\sigma_x^2 + 2\sigma_{x\phi} + \sigma_\phi^2 \right).$$

Then, given that $E \left(\phi^*_{t,T} \right) = e^{\mu_\phi + \frac{1}{2}\sigma_\phi^2} = 1$, we have [44]

$$\ln E \left(x_{t+T} \phi^*_{t,t+T} \right) = \mu_x + \frac{1}{2}\sigma_x^2 + \sigma_{x\phi}$$

and the futures price is

$$H_{t,t+T} = e^{\mu_x + \frac{1}{2}\sigma_x^2 + \sigma_{x\phi}}. \tag{6.8}$$

This expression for the futures price of an asset, derived in a multi-period rational expectations model, is similar to the the formula for the forward price derived in Chapter 3, in the case of the single-period model. The difference is that here, the product of the pricing kernels is $\phi^*_{t,t+T}$, whereas in Chapter 3, the single-period pricing kernel was $\phi_{t,t+T}$. Hence, in the lognormal case, the multi-period futures price has a similar *form* to that of the forward price in the single-period model.

---

[43] This follows from the fact that $\phi^*_{t,t+T}$ is known at time $t + T$.
[44] This, in turn, follows from the fact that $E_\tau(\phi_{\tau,\tau+1)} = 1$ for all τ, see Exercise 6.4.

In the appendix to Chapter 3, we showed that if X and Y are lognormal with $X = \mathrm{e}^x$ and $Y = \mathrm{e}^y$, it follows that

$$\mathrm{cov}\,(X, Y) = E\,(X)\,E\,(Y)\,(1 - \mathrm{e}^{\sigma_{xy}}),$$

where σ_{xy} is the covariance of x and y. We can now use this result to analyse the forward-futures bias. We assume that $x_{t+T}, \phi^*_{t,t+T}$ and $b_{t,t+T}$ are multi-variate lognormal variables. It then follows that the forward price of $x_{t,t+T}$ is

$$
\begin{aligned}
F_{t,t+T} &= E_t\left(x_{t+T}\phi^*_{t,t+T}b_{t,t+T}\right) \\
&= E_t\left(x_{t+T}\right)E_t\left(\phi^*_{t,t+T}b_{t,t+T}\right) + \mathrm{cov}\left(x_{t+T},\ \phi^*_{t,t+T}b_{t,t+T}\right) \\
&= E_t\left(x_{t+T}\right)\mathrm{e}^{\mathrm{cov}\left(\ln x_{t+T},\ \ln \phi^*_{t,t+T}b_{t,t+T}\right)}
\end{aligned}
$$

since $E_t\left(\phi^*_{t,t+T}b_{t,t+T}\right) = 1$.[45]

Given that $E_t\left(x_{t+T}\right) = \mathrm{e}^{\mu_x + \frac{1}{2}\sigma_x^2}$, let $\sigma_{x\phi}$ denote $\mathrm{cov}\left(\ln x_{t+T},\ \ln \phi^*_{t,t+T}\right)$ and σ_{xb} denote $\mathrm{cov}(\ln x_{t+T},\ \ln b_{t,t+T})$, it then follows that the forward price is given by

$$F_{t,t+T} = \mathrm{e}^{\mu_x + \frac{1}{2}\sigma_x^2}\mathrm{e}^{\sigma_{x\phi} + \sigma_{xb}}.$$

Finally, using (6.8) we find

$$F_{t,t+T} = H_{t,t+T}\mathrm{e}^{\sigma_{xb}}. \tag{6.9}$$

To evaluate the forward-futures difference, we first write $\sigma_{xb} = \sigma_x\sigma_b\rho_{xb}$. Now we see that (a) if interest rate are non-stochastic; $\sigma_b = 0$, or (b) if interest rates are uncorrelated with x_{t+T}; $\rho_{xb} = 0$. For these two special cases, $\sigma_{xb} = 0$, $\mathrm{e}^{\sigma_{xb}} = 1$ and the forward price will be the same as futures price. Suppose now that the cash flow, x_{t+T} is itself a bond price, so that the forward contract is a forward on a bond. In this case we can presume that the covariance between the x_{t+T} and the discount factor $b_{t,t+T}$ is positive. In this case, $\mathrm{e}^{\sigma_{xb}} > 1$, and the forward price of the bond will exceed its futures price. We explore this example further in the following section, for the special case where x_{t+T} is a short-term zero-coupon bond.

---

[45] See Exercise 6.1 and Chapter 3, appendix.

6.5   Futures Rates and Forward Rates in a Normal Interest-Rate Model

We now consider the case where x_{t+T} is the price of a one-period zero-coupon bond: $B_{t+T,t+T+1} = e^{-r_{t+T}}$, where r_{t+T} is the one period spot rate at time $t+T$. We assume that the r_{t+T} is normally distributed and hence the bond price, $B_{t+T,t+T+1}$, is lognormally distributed. With r_{t+T} being normal, we denote $E_t(-r_{t+T}) = \mu_x$, and $\text{var}_t(r_{t+T}) = \sigma_x^2$. The long futures contract on the bond allows one to purchase the bond, at $H_{t,t+T}$. Further, let the futures rate be defined by the relationship:[46]

$$H_{t,t+T} = e^{-h_{t,t+T}}.$$

Similarly, let $F_{t,t+T}$ be the forward price, with $f_{t,t+T}$ the forward rate where

$$F_{t,t+T} = e^{-f_{t,t+T}}.$$

Then, we have, using equation (6.9),

$$\ln\left(\frac{F_{t,t+T}}{H_{t,t+T}}\right) = h_{t,t+T} - f_{t,t+T} = \sigma_{xb}, \qquad (6.10)$$

where

$$\sigma_{xb} = \text{cov}\left[\ln\left(B_{t+T,t+T+1}\right), \ln b_{t,t+T}\right]$$

and $\ln b_{t,t+T} = \ln\left[(B_{t,t+1}B_{t+1,t+2}\cdots B_{t+T-1,t+T})/B_{t,t+T}\right]$. Note here that the terms $\ln B_{t,t+1}$ and $\ln B_{t,T}$ are non-stochastic, given that we are standing at time t. It then follows that

$$\sigma_{xb} = \text{cov}\left[r_{t+T}, (r_{t+1} + r_{t+2} + \cdots + r_{t+T-1})\right],$$

since $B_{\tau,\tau+1} = e^{-r_\tau}$. Hence, it follows that

$$\sigma_{xb} = \sum_{\tau=1}^{T-1} \text{cov}\left(r_{t+\tau}, r_{t+T}\right).$$

Assuming that the covariances are positive, then $\sigma_{xb} > 0$ and the futures rate is greater than the forward rate from (6.10).

---

[46] Note that the futures rate $h_{t,t+T}$ here is defined differently from the *LIBOR* market convention. See Chapter 7 for an analysis of futures and forward rates when rates are defined using the *LIBOR* market convention.

In the case of a single factor interest-rate model, where the interest rate follows a random walk such that $r_{\tau+1} = r_\tau + \varepsilon_\tau$ and $\text{cov}\,(r_\tau, r_{\tau+1}) = \text{var}\,(r_\tau)$, the futures rate is greater than the forward rate, and the difference widens when T gets larger.

6.6 Futures and Forward Prices of European-style Contingent Claims

In Chapter 3, we priced European-style contingent claims under the assumption that the underling asset price and the pricing kernel were joint-lognormal. Here we extend this analysis to determine the futures and forward prices of these claims. It turns out that the difference between the futures and forward prices is magnified considerably when the options are written on interest-rate dependent securities. The futures price of an option is relevant for European-style options that are marked to market. Such options are traded on the London International financial futures exchange (LIFFE).

Let $H_{t,t+T}[g(x_{t+T})]$ denote the futures price of a contingent claim paying $g\,(x_{t+T})$ at time $t + T$. Taking the expectation of the payoff under the risk-neutral measure as in (6.4), the futures price of the claim is

$$H_{t,t+T}[g(x_{t+T})] = E^Q[g(x_{t+T})].$$

Re-writing this in terms of the pricing kernels:

$$H_{t,t+T}\,[g\,(x_{t+T})] = E_t\,\big[\phi^*_{t,t+T}\,g\,(x_{t+T})\big]$$
$$= E_t\,\big[g\,(x_{t+T})\,E_t\,\big(\phi^*_{t,t+T}|x_{t+T}\big)\big]\,.$$

As in Chapter 3, the conditional expectation of the pricing kernel, $E_t\,\big(\phi^*_{t,t+T}\,|\,x_{t+T}\big)$, is the asset-specific pricing kernel, $\psi^*_{t,t+T}$. Now, assuming that x_{t+T} and $\phi^*_{t,t+T}$ are joint-lognormal, we proceed using the same method as in Chapter 3. We now write the futures price of the option as the integral:

$$H_{t,t+T}\,[g\,(x_{t+T})] = \int_{-\infty}^{\infty} g\,(x_{t+T})\,\psi^*_{t,t+T}\frac{1}{\sigma_x\sqrt{2\pi}}e^{-\frac{1}{2\sigma_x^2}(\ln x - \mu_x)^2}\,\mathrm{d}\ln x.$$

$$(6.11)$$

We now substitute the futures price of the underlying asset, in order to derive a RNVR. Given the joint-lognormality of $\phi^*_{t,t+T}$

and x_{t+T}, the futures price of the underlying asset is, from above

$$H_{t,t+T} = e^{\mu_x + \frac{1}{2}\sigma_x^2 + \sigma_{x\phi}}.$$

Using a similar argument to that employed in Chapter 3, the conditional pricing kernel is

$$\psi_{t,t+T}^* = e^{-\mu_x \beta - \frac{1}{2}\beta^2 \sigma_x^2} \left(x_{t+T}\right)^\beta ,$$

and equation (6.11) can be written as

$$H_{t,t+T} \left[g\left(x_{t+T}\right)\right] = \int_{-\infty}^{\infty} g\left(x_{t+T}\right)$$

$$\times \frac{1}{\sigma_x \sqrt{2\pi}} e^{-\frac{1}{2\sigma_x^2}\left[\ln x - \left(\ln H_{t,t+T} - \frac{1}{2}\sigma_x^2\right)\right]^2} \, d\ln x.$$

As in the one-period option valuation model in Chapter 3, we have derived a RNVR for the option price. Here the RNVR exists between the *futures* price of the contingent claim and the *futures* price of the underlying asset. The resulting option pricing model, in the case of a European-style call or put option, is often referred to as the Black model.[47]

We now derive the *forward* price of a European-style contingent claim. Using the above definition of $b_{t,t+T}$

$$b_{t,t+T} = \frac{B_{t,t+1}\widetilde{B}_{t+1,t+2}\cdots\widetilde{B}_{T-1,T}}{B_{t,T}},$$

where $B_{\tau,\tau+1} = e^{-r_\tau}$. We now assume that r_τ has a normal distribution, so that bond prices is lognormal.[48] It follows that $b_{t,t+T}$ is lognormal. Then defining $\phi_{t,t+T} = \phi_{t,t+T}^* b_{t,t+T}$ and proceeding to value the contingent claim using the same method as in the case of the futures price of the option, we find after substituting the forward price of the underlying asset,

$$F_{t,t+T} = e^{\mu_x + \frac{1}{2}\sigma_x^2 + \sigma_{x\phi} + \sigma_{xb}},$$

---

[47] There are many versions of the Black model, however. The Black model is also used with forward prices or forward interest rates substituted for the futures price of the underlying asset. See, for example, Hull (2003).

[48] Note that in general, this is not a very good assumption because it allows interest rates to become negative. However, here we are not pricing interest-rate options, merely using the interest rate as a discount rate.

and the forward price of the option is

$$F_{t,t+T}\left[g\left(x_{t+T}\right)\right] = \int_{-\infty}^{\infty} g\left(x_{t+T}\right)$$

$$\times \frac{1}{\sigma_x\sqrt{2\pi}} e^{-\frac{1}{2\sigma_x^2}\left[\ln x - \left(\ln F_{t,t+T} - \frac{1}{2}\sigma_x^2\right)\right]^2} \mathrm{d}\ln x.$$

Again, a RNVR exists for the price of the contingent claim. In this case, however the RNVR is between the *forward* price of the claim and the *forward* price of the underlying asset. Note that the forward price and the futures price of the claim will be the same as the futures price in a one-period world. However, in the multi-period world, with stochastic interest rates, the difference between futures price of a call option and forward price of a call option, for example is

$$H_{t,t+T}\left[g\left(x_{t+T}\right)\right] - F_{t,t+T}\left[g\left(x_{t+T}\right)\right]$$

$$= \int_{-\infty}^{\infty} \left(x_{t+T} - K\right) \widehat{f}\left(x_{t+T}\right) \mathrm{d}x_{t+T}$$

$$- \int_{-\infty}^{\infty} \left(x_{t+T} - K\right) f^*\left(x_{t+T}\right) \mathrm{d}x_{t+T},$$

where $\widehat{f}\left(x_{t+T}\right) \sim N\left[\ln H_{t,t+T}, \sigma\right]$ and $f^*\left(x_{t+T}\right) \sim N\left[\ln F_{t,t+T}, \sigma\right]$.

6.7   Conclusions and Further Reading

In this chapter, we have applied the multi-period rational expectations approach developed in Chapter 5, to analyse the difference between the forward and futures prices of assets and contingent claims. Often forward and futures prices are treated as equivalent in treatments of financial theory. However, for some claims the difference is highly significant. These are claims on assets that are closely related to interest rates. Also, when we consider the futures and forward prices of contingent claims these can differ considerably. The development here is closest to that found in Pliska (1997). In that treatment the author extends the analysis of contingent claims to American-style contingent claims. Further discussion of the forward and futures prices of contingent claims can be found in Hull (2003).

Exercises

6.1 (a) Suppose X and Y are joint-lognormal. Prove that
$$E\left(XY\right) = E\left(X\right)E\left(Y\right)\mathrm{e}^{\sigma_{xy}}.$$

(b) show that, when x_{t+T}, $\phi_{t,t+T}$ and $b_{t,t+T}$ are multivariate lognormal
$$\mathrm{cov}_t^Q\left(x_{t+T}, b_{t,t+T}\right) = H_{t,t+T}\left(\mathrm{e}^{\sigma_{xb}} - 1\right).$$

6.2 (a) Given
$$E\left(\phi \mid x\right) = \mathrm{e}^{-\mu_x \beta - \frac{1}{2}\beta^2 \sigma_x^2}\left(\frac{x}{S}\right)^\beta$$

and that
$$H_{t,t+T} = \mathrm{e}^{\mu_x + \frac{1}{2}\sigma_x^2 + \sigma_{x\phi}}.$$

show that a RNVR holds for the futures price of a contingent claim.

(b) Show that $E\left(\phi \mid x\right)$ lognormal is necessary for a RNVR to hold for $H_{t,t+T}\left[b\left(x_{t+T}\right)\right]$.

6.3 Assume that the variance of a one-year zero-coupon bond is $\sigma_x^2 = (5)(0.01)^2$ and that the covariance
$$\sigma_{xb} = \frac{T\left(T-1\right)}{2}\left(0.01\right)^2.$$

If the futures rate is 0.06 (for one-year money), what is
(a) the futures price?
(b) the forward rate?
(c) the forward price?

6.4 Given the definition of $\phi_{t,t+T}^*$ in Section 6.4, show that
$$E_t(\phi_{t,t+T}^*) = 1.$$

6.5 Assume that $t = 0$, $T = 2$ and the zero-coupon bond prices are $B_{0,1}$ and $B_{0,2}$. Let the futures price be $H_{0,2}$ and the spot price at time 2 be S_2. Illustrate a self-financing strategy which can turn $H_{0,2}$ into $S_2/(B_{0,1}B_{1,2})$.

BOND PRICING, INTEREST-RATE PROCESSES, AND THE LIBOR MARKET MODEL

Bond pricing is an important application of the rational expectations approach to valuation. Long-term bond prices and bond forward prices can be obtained by taking appropriate expected values of future spot pries, under the risk-neutral measure. In this chapter we use the complete market, pricing kernel approach to value bonds, given stochastic interest rates. One important, practical problem is to model bond prices and interest rates with the correct drifts. This is required in order to value interest-rate derivatives. We derive here the drift of the bond prices and interest rates under the period-by-period risk-neutral measure. As a special case, we then take the case of interest rates defined on a London Interbank Offer Rate (LIBOR) basis. We derive the drift of forward rates in what is generally known as the LIBOR market model.

7.1 Bond Pricing under Rational Expectations

In the previous chapter we used the rational expectations approach to value a cash flow x_{t+T} which occurs at time $t + T$. Its value at time t is given by

$$
\begin{aligned}
S_t = E_t \Bigg\{ \phi_{t,t+1} E_{t+1} \Bigg[\phi_{t+1,t+2} \cdots \\
E_{t+T-1} \left(\phi_{t+T-1,t+T} \prod_{\tau=0}^{T-1} B_{t+\tau,t+\tau+1} x_{t+T} \right) \Bigg] \Bigg\}.
\end{aligned} \tag{7.1}
$$

In order to value a bond paying certain cash flows, we first take the case where $x_{t+n} = \$1$ in every state and $t + n$ is the maturity date of the bond. The value of the cash flow in this case is hence

$$B_{t,t+n} = E_t \left\{ \phi_{t,t+1} E_{t+1} \left[\phi_{t+1,t+2} \cdots \right. \right.$$

$$\left. \left. E_{t+n-1} \left(\phi_{t+n-1,t+n} \prod_{\tau=0}^{n-1} B_{t+\tau,t+\tau+1} \right) \right] \right\}. \qquad (7.2)$$

This is the value of a zero-coupon bond which has n periods to maturity. As in the previous chapter it is often convenient to write this as an expectation under the 'risk-neutral' measure:

$$B_{t,t+n} = E_t^Q \left\{ E_{t+1}^Q \left[E_{t+2}^Q \cdots \left(\prod_{\tau=0}^{n-1} B_{t+\tau,t+\tau+1} \right) \right] \right\} \qquad (7.3)$$

or, simply, using the property of expectations,

$$B_{t,t+n} = E_t^Q \left(\prod_{\tau=0}^{n-1} B_{t+\tau,t+\tau+1} \right). \qquad (7.4)$$

Equation (7.3) expresses the value of a long-term bond as an expectation of future stochastic short-term bond prices. We can now use equation (7.4) to obtain a further important result. First note that (7.4) can be written as:

$$B_{t,t+n} = B_{t,t+1} E_t^Q \left[E_{t+1}^Q \left(\prod_{\tau=1}^{n-1} B_{t+\tau,t+\tau+1} \right) \right]$$

$$= B_{t,t+1} E_t^Q \left(B_{t+1,t+n} \right),$$

since $B_{t,t+1}$ is non-stochastic. Hence dividing through by $B_{t,t+1}$ we have, using spot-forward parity,

$$F_{t,t+1,t+n} = \frac{B_{t,t+n}}{B_{t,t+1}}$$

$$= E_t^Q \left[B_{t+1,t+n} \right].$$

This states that the (one-period-ahead) forward price of a bond is the expectation, under the Q measure, of the (one-period-ahead) spot price of the bond.[49]

---

[49] It is important to note that this is only true for the one-period-ahead prices.

These pricing equations will now be used to analyse the forward prices of bonds, and in particular the drift, or expected increase, of forward prices.

7.1.1   Bond Forward Prices

In the table below, we present the spot prices and forward prices of a zero-coupon bond which pays \$1 at time $t + n$. The forward contract matures at time $t + T < t + n$. In the first part of the table we show the spot and forward prices using the $\widetilde{B}$ and $\widetilde{F}$ notation to emphasise the fact that these prices are stochastic. The zero-coupon bond prices converge to \$1 at time $t + n$. The forward prices for delivery of the bond at time $t + T$ converge to the spot price $\widetilde{B}_{t+T,t+n}$ at time $t + T$.

Bond prices and bond forward prices

t	$t+1$	$t+T$	... $t+n$
$B_{t,t+n}$	$\widetilde{B}_{t+1,t+n}$	$\widetilde{B}_{t+T,t+n}$ ...	\$1
$F_{t,t+T,t+n} \rightarrow$	$\widetilde{F}_{t+1,t+T,t+n} \rightarrow$	$\widetilde{B}_{t+T,t+n}$	
$F_{t,t+T,t+n} =$	$E_t^Q(\widetilde{F}_{t+1,t+T,t+n})+$		
	$\mathrm{cov}_t^Q(F_{t+1,t+T,t+n}, B_{t+1,t+T})\frac{B_{t,t+1}}{B_{t,t+T}}$		

In the second part of the table we state a result that the T-period forward price of the bond at time t equals the expected forward price at $t+1$ plus a term whose sign depends on the covariance (under the Q measure) of the time $t+1$ bond price and bond forward price. Since this covariance is likely to be positive, this result shows that the drift of the forward bond price under the Q measure:

$$E_t^Q(F_{t+1,t+T,t+n}) - F_{t,t+T,t+n}$$

$$= -\frac{B_{t,t+1}}{B_{t,t+T}}\mathrm{cov}_t^Q(F_{t+1,t+T,t+n}, B_{t+1,t+T}) \qquad (7.5)$$

is likely to be negative. In the following argument we establish this fundamental result.

First, we use forward parity to write the bond price at time $t+1$:

$$B_{t+1,t+n} = F_{t+1,t+T,t+n}B_{t+1,t+T}.$$

Next, we take the expected value and use the definition of covariance to obtain

$$E_t^Q[B_{t+1,t+n}] = E_t^Q[F_{t+1,t+T,t+n}]E_t^Q[B_{t+1,t+T}]$$
$$+ \operatorname{cov}_t^Q(F_{t+1,t+T,t+n}, B_{t+1,t+T}).$$

Now, using the result derived above that the one-period-ahead forward bond price is the expected value, under the Q measure of the one-period-ahead spot bond price, we can write

$$\frac{B_{t,t+n}}{B_{t,t+1}} = E_t^Q[F_{t+1,t+T,t+n}]\frac{B_{t,t+T}}{B_{t,t+1}}$$
$$+ \operatorname{cov}_t^Q(F_{t+1,t+T,t+n}, B_{t+1,t+T}).$$

Then, equation (7.5) follows immediately by multiplying by $B_{t,t+1}$ and dividing by $B_{t,t+T}$.

7.1.2   Some Further Implications of Forward Parity and Rational Expectations

One special case of the drift in (7.5) above is the case where $T = 1$. Here equation (7.5) simplifies to

$$F_{t,t+1,t+n} = E_t^Q(B_{t+1,t+n}), \tag{7.6}$$

since $F_{t+1,t+1,t+n} = B_{t+1,t+n}$ and $B_{t+1,t+1} = 1$, a constant. Hence, the one-period ahead forward price of the n-period bond is just the expected value of the subsequent period spot price of the bond. We now apply forward parity arguments to expand the right- and left-hand sides of equation (7.6).

First, the spot price at $t+1$ on the right-hand side of (7.6) can be written as:

$$B_{t+1,t+n} = B_{t+1,t+2}F_{t+1,t+2,t+n}F_{t+1,t+3,t+n}...F_{t+1,t+n-1,t+n},$$
$$\tag{7.7}$$

i.e., the spot price is the product of successive forward prices. Also, using a similar argument the left-hand side of (7.6) can be written as:

$$F_{t,t+1,t+n} = F_{t,t+1,t+2}F_{t,t+2,t+3}\cdots F_{t,t+n-1,t+n}. \tag{7.8}$$

This follows from the fact that a long-term forward contract can be replicated by a series of short-term contracts.

7.2 The Drift of Forward Rates

One of the challenges of financial theory has been to construct dynamic models of the term structure of interest rates which are consistent with no-arbitrage. In order to achieve this, models have to satisfy the condition derived above that bond forward prices for all maturities equal the expectations of the one-period-ahead spot bond prices for those maturities, under the risk-neutral measure. However, in order to price interest-rate dependent derivatives, often what is required is a model of the evolution of forward interest rates rather than forward prices. In this section, we therefore derive the correct drift of the forward interest rate.

Interest rates can be expressed in many different ways. In this chapter we use the conventional annual rate. For simplicity, assume that the period length, from t to $t+1$ is one year. The annual yield rate at time t, y_t, is then defined by the equation

$$B_{t,t+1} = \frac{1}{1 + y_t}.$$

Consistent with this spot yield rate we define the forward rate at time t, as $f_{t,t+T}$, in the equation

$$F_{t,t+T,t+T+1} = \frac{1}{1 + f_{t,t+T}}.$$

Note that we will always refer to forward rates for one-year loans and hence we have dropped the final subscript on the forward rate.

Using these definitions and substituting (7.7) and (7.8) in the equation (7.6), we find the following:

$$
\begin{aligned}
& E_t^Q \left[\frac{1}{1 + y_{t+1}} \frac{1}{1 + f_{t+1,t+2}} \cdots \frac{1}{1 + f_{t+T-1,t+T}} \right] \\
& = \frac{1}{1 + f_{t,t+1}} \frac{1}{1 + f_{t,t+2}} \cdots \frac{1}{1 + f_{t,t+T}}.
\end{aligned}
\tag{7.9}
$$

Note that equation (7.9) holds for all values of T. Hence, in particular, with $T = 1$,

$$E_t^Q \left[\frac{1}{1 + y_{t+1}} \right] = \frac{1}{1 + f_{t,t+1}}.
\tag{7.10}$$

These relationships will play a key role in our subsequent derivation of the forward rate drift.

We now ask the question: what is the drift of the forward rate, $f_{t,t+T}$, under the risk-neutral measure? That is, what is $E_t^Q[f_{t+1,t+T}] - f_{t,t+T}$? To answer the question, we introduce the following contract definition.

Definition 6 *A forward rate agreement (FRA) is an agreement made at time t to exchange fixed-rate interest payments at a rate k for variable rate payments, on a principal amount A, for the loan period $t + T$ to $t + T + 1$.*

The time scale for payments on a T-maturity FRA is shown below:

$$Ay_{t+T}$$
$$\downarrow$$

$$t \text{ ———— } t+T \text{ ———— } t+T+1$$

$$\uparrow$$
$$-Ak$$

Here, t is the contract agreement date, $t + T$ is the settlement date, and $t + T + 1$ is the date on which the notional loan underlying the FRA is repaid.

The contract is usually settled in cash at $t + T$ on a discounted basis. The settlement amount at time $t + T$ on a long FRA is

$$FRA_{t+T} = \frac{A\,(y_{t+T} - k)}{1 + y_{t+T}}.$$

From here onwards, for convenience we assume that the principal $A = \$1$. Note that the FRA settlement takes place at $t + T$, and is discounted by the spot rate discount factor $1/(1 + y_{t+T})$. In contrast, a futures contract on an interest rate payoff would not be discounted, although it is also settled at $t + T$. At the time of the contract inception, an FRA is normally structured so that it has zero value. To gaurantee this, the strike rate k is set equal to the market forward rate $f_{t,t+T}$. We denote the value of the FRA at time t as $FRA_{t,t+T}$. Hence, if the FRA is correctly priced we must have:

$$FRA_{t,t+T} = E_t^Q\left(\frac{y_{t+T} - f_{t,t+T}}{1 + y_{t+T}}\right) = 0. \tag{7.11}$$

Note again that equation (7.11) holds for all forward maturities T. Given a probability distribution of possible outcomes of the interest rate y_{t+T}, the equation determines the market forward rate, $f_{t,t+T}$.

7.2.1 FRA Pricing and the Drift of the Forward Rate: One-period Case

The determination of $f_{t,t+T}$ is complicated by the fact that the FRA payment is discounted over successive periods at the stochastic rate of interest. The argument is easier to understand, if we start initially with a one-period FRA and then proceed to price a two-period FRA, before moving to the general T-period case.

We first consider a one-year FRA. Since a one-period FRA struck at $f_{t,t+1}$ has zero value, employing equation (7.11), with $T = 1$, we have

$$E_t^Q \left(\frac{y_{t+1} - f_{t,t+1}}{1 + y_{t+1}} \right) = 0,$$

and it follows that

$$E_t^Q \left(\frac{f_{t,t+1}}{1 + y_{t+1}} \right) = E_t^Q \left(\frac{y_{t+1}}{1 + y_{t+1}} \right)$$

and hence that

$$f_{t,t+1} E_t^Q \left(\frac{1}{1 + y_{t+1}} \right) = E_t^Q (y_{t+1}) E_t^Q \left(\frac{1}{1 + y_{t+1}} \right)$$
$$+ \mathrm{cov}_t^Q \left(y_{t+1}, \frac{1}{1 + y_{t+1}} \right).$$

One problem in evaluating this equation is the term $E_t^Q [1/(1 + y_{t+1})]$. However, we can now use the result from equation (7.9) with $T = 1$ to write

$$E_t^Q \left(\frac{1}{1 + y_{t+1}} \right) = \frac{1}{1 + f_{t,t+1}}$$

and it follows, multiplying by $(1 + f_{t,t+1})$,

$$E_t^Q (y_{t+1}) - f_{t,t+1} = -(1 + f_{t,t+1}) \mathrm{cov}_t^Q \left(y_{t+1}, \frac{1}{1 + y_{t+1}} \right).$$
$$(7.12)$$

Equation (7.12) shows that the drift of the forward rate is determined by a covariance term involving y_{t+1} and a function of y_{t+1}. As y_{t+1} increases, $1/(1 + y_{t+1})$ decreases. Hence, the covariance term is negative and the drift of the forward rate $E_t^Q(y_{t+1}) - f_{t,t+1}$ is always positive.

7.2.2 FRA Pricing and the Drift of the Forward Rate: Two-period Case

We now proceed to calculate the drift of a two-period forward rate over the first period. We use a similar argument, but this time consider a two-period FRA. At time t, assume that we enter a long two-period maturity FRA contract with a strike price k_1. The expected payoff at the maturity date, $t + 2$ is

$$\frac{y_{t+2} - k_1}{1 + y_{t+2}}.$$

Under no-arbitrage, the strike rate must equal the two-year forward rate, i.e., $k_1 = f_{t,t+2}$. At the end of the first period, we enter a short FRA contract (i.e., this is known as a reversal strategy) with the following payoff

$$\frac{k_2 - y_{t+2}}{1 + y_{t+2}},$$

again at time $t + 2$. Under no arbitrage, the strike rate on this second FRA must equal the one-period-ahead forward rate at $t + 1$, i.e., $k_2 = f_{t+1,t+2}$. Now we evaluate the portfolio of the original FRA plus the short FRA entered into at $t + 1$. Substituting for k_1 and k_2, the payoff on the portfolio at time $t + 2$ is given by

$$\frac{f_{t+1,t+2} - f_{t,t+2}}{1 + y_{t+2}},$$

since the uncertain interest rate, y_{t+2}, in the numerator cancels out.

The value of the portfolio at time $t + 1$ is found by taking the expected value at $t + 1$, under the Q measure and discounting by the interest rate y_{t+1}. This is

$$E_{t+1}^Q \left(\frac{f_{t+1,t+2} - f_{t,t+2}}{1 + y_{t+2}} \right) \frac{1}{1 + y_{t+1}}$$

$$= (f_{t+1,t+2} - f_{t,t+2}) E_{t+1}^Q \left(\frac{1}{1 + y_{t+2}} \right) \frac{1}{1 + y_{t+1}}$$

$$= (f_{t+1,t+2} - f_{t,t+2}) \frac{1}{1 + f_{t+1,t+2}} \frac{1}{1 + y_{t+1}}, \qquad (7.13)$$

where the last equation follows from taking (7.10), with $n = 2$. Finally, evaluating the value of the portfolio back at time t using (7.13), we must have

$$E_t^Q \left(\frac{f_{t+1,t+2} - f_{t,t+2}}{1 + f_{t+1,t+2}} \frac{1}{1 + y_{t+1}} \right) = 0,$$

and hence

$$E_t^Q \left(\frac{f_{t+1,t+2}}{1 + f_{t+1,t+2}} \frac{1}{1 + y_{t+1}} \right) = f_{t,t+2} E_t^Q \left(\frac{1}{1 + f_{t+1,t+2}} \frac{1}{1 + y_{t+1}} \right).$$

It then follows that the drift of the two-period forward rate is given by

$$E_t^Q (f_{t+1,t+2}) - f_{t,t+2}$$

$$= -\text{cov}_t^Q \left(f_{t+1,t+2}, \frac{1}{1 + y_{t+1}} \frac{1}{1 + f_{t+1,t+2}} \right)$$

$$\times (1 + f_{t,t+1})(1 + f_{t,t+2}). \qquad (7.14)$$

To obtain the last term in (7.14) we have used (7.9) with $T = 2$. In general the drift of the T-period forward rate

$$E_t^Q (f_{t+1,t+T}) - f_{t,t+T}$$

$$= -\text{cov}_t^Q \left(f_{t+1,t+T}, \frac{1}{1 + y_{t+1}} \cdots \frac{1}{1 + f_{t+1,t+T}} \right)$$

$$\times (1 + f_{t,t+1}) \cdots (1 + f_{t,t+T}). \qquad (7.15)$$

To obtain the last term in (7.15) we have again used (7.9). In general, the covariance term in equation (7.15) is difficult to evaluate. However, if the one-period ahead spot rates and forward rates are assumed to be lognormal, the covariance can be easily evaluated in terms of logarithmic covariances. This leads to a model that can be implemented easily and practically.

7.2.3 The Drift of the Forward Rate under Lognormality

We now assume that the forward rate $f_{t+1,t+T}$ is lognormal for all forward maturities, T. We can then evaluate the covariance term, using an approximation. In the appendix, we show that the following approximation holds for the covariance of two variables X and Y, by expanding X around a constant a and Y around a constant b:

$$\operatorname{cov}(X, Y) \approx ab \operatorname{cov}(\ln X, \ln Y).$$

We now evaluate the drift of the yield rate in (7.12), assuming that y_{t+1} is lognormal. Here we take $a = f_{t,t+1}$ and $b = 1/(1 + f_{t,t+1})$. We then have

$$\operatorname{cov}_t^Q\left(y_{t+1}, \frac{1}{1 + y_{t+1}}\right)$$
$$= f_{t,t+1}\left(\frac{1}{1 + f_{t,t+1}}\right)\operatorname{cov}_t^Q\left(\ln y_{t+1}, \ln \frac{1}{1 + y_{t+1}}\right)$$

and substituting in (7.12), the drift of the one-year forward rate is

$$E_t^Q(y_{t+1}) - f_{t,t+1} = -f_{t,t+1}\operatorname{cov}_t^Q\left(\ln y_{t+1}, \ln \frac{1}{1 + y_{t+1}}\right). \quad (7.16)$$

We now proceed to evaluate the drift of the two-year forward rate in equation (7.14). Here we have the term

$$\operatorname{cov}_t^Q\left(f_{t+1,t+2}, \frac{1}{1 + y_{t+1}} \frac{1}{1 + f_{t+1,t+2}}\right)$$
$$= f_{t,t+2}\operatorname{cov}_t^Q\left[\ln f_{t+1,t+2}, \ln\left(\frac{1}{1 + y_{t+1}} \frac{1}{1 + f_{t+1,t+2}}\right)\right]$$
$$\times \frac{1}{(1 + f_{t,t+1})(1 + f_{t,t+2})}.$$

Substituting this in the first part of equation (7.14) and using the property of logarithms we find that

$$
E_t^Q \left[f_{t+1,t+2} \right] - f_{t,t+2} = - f_{t,t+2} \mathrm{cov}_t^Q \left(\ln f_{t+1,t+2}, \ln \frac{1}{1+y_{t+1}} \right)
$$

$$
- f_{t,t+2} \mathrm{cov}_t^Q \left(\ln f_{t+1,t+2}, \ln \frac{1}{1+f_{t+1,t+2}} \right).
$$

$$(7.17)$$

In general, the drift of the T-maturity forward rate depends on the sum of a series of covariance terms. The drift in the general case is

$$
E_t^Q \left(f_{t+1,t+T} \right) - f_{t,t+T}
$$

$$
= - f_{t,t+T} \mathrm{cov}_t^Q \left(\ln f_{t+1,t+T}, \ln \frac{1}{1+y_{t+1}} \right)
$$

$$
- \cdots - f_{t,t+T} \mathrm{cov}_t^Q \left(\ln f_{t+1,t+T}, \ln \frac{1}{1+f_{t+1,t+T}} \right).
$$

$$(7.18)$$

Finally, in order to state the covariance terms in a more recognisable form, we use Stein's lemma to evaluate the terms with a form

$$
\mathrm{cov}_t^Q \left(\ln f_{t+1,t+T}, \ln \frac{1}{1+f_{t+1,t+2}} \right),
$$

for example. In the appendix (at the end of this chapter), we show that if X and Y are joint-lognormal variables then

$$
\mathrm{cov} \left[\ln X, \ln \left(\frac{1}{1+Y} \right) \right] = E \left(\frac{-Y}{1+Y} \right) \mathrm{cov} \left(\ln X, \ln Y \right).
$$

This follows from an extension of Stein's lemma, which was used in chapter 1 to derive the CAPM. Using $X = f_{t+1,t+T}$ and $Y = f_{t+1,t+2}$, we have

$$
\mathrm{cov}_t^Q \left(\ln f_{t+1,t+T}, \ln \frac{1}{1+f_{t+1,t+2}} \right)
$$

$$
= E_t^Q \left(\frac{-f_{t+1,t+2}}{1+f_{t+1,t+2}} \right) \mathrm{cov}_t^Q \left(\ln f_{t+1,t+T}, \ln f_{t+1,t+2} \right).
$$

Finally, substituting similar expressions in the drift equation (7.18) and using the relation:[50]

$$E_t^Q \left(\frac{f_{t+1,t+T}}{1 + f_{t+1,t+T}} \right) = \frac{f_{t,t+T}}{1 + f_{t,t+T}}$$

gives

$$E_t^Q \left(f_{t+1,t+T} \right) - f_{t,t+T}$$

$$= f_{t,t+T} \frac{f_{t,t+1}}{1 + f_{t,t+1}} \operatorname{cov}_t^Q \left(\ln f_{t+1,t+T}, \ln f_{t+1,t+1} \right)$$

$$+ \cdots + f_{t,t+T} \frac{f_{t,t+T}}{1 + f_{t,t+T}} \operatorname{cov}_t^Q \left(\ln f_{t+1,t+T}, \ln f_{t+1,t+T} \right).$$

In this model, the drift of the forward rate over the first period depends on the logarithmic covariances of the forward rates.

7.3   An Application of the Forward Rate Drift: The LIBOR Market Model

The LIBOR is a short-term interest rate quoted for a period less than or equal to one year. The most important rate is the three-month US Dollar LIBOR. Most interest-rate derivative contracts, FRAs for example, are contracts on LIBOR. Let $f_{t,t+T}$ denote the T-period forward LIBOR at time t. Following market convention, $f_{t,t+T}$ is quoted as a simple annual rate. The relationship of the forward price of a zero-coupon bond to the quoted rate is given by

$$F_{t,t+T,t+T+\delta} = \frac{1}{1 + \delta f_{t,t+T}},$$

where δ is length of the loan period, or re-set interval. If $T = 0$, $f_{t,t}$ is the spot LIBOR, where

$$F_{t,t,t+\delta} = B_{t,t+\delta} = \frac{1}{1 + \delta f_{t,t}}.$$

In this section, we derive the drift of the forward rate: $f_{t,t+T}$, when it is quoted on a LIBOR basis. We make the assumption that forward rates, in one period's time, are joint lognormally distributed, for all maturities T. With this assumption, we can use the results

---

[50] This follows from the pricing of a T-maturity FRA.

of the previous section, merely substituting the LIBOR for the annual yield rate. Also, since time is now measured in δ intervals, the settlement payment for an FRA on LIBOR is given by

$$\text{FRA}_{t+T} = \frac{A\left(f_{t+T,t+T} - k\right)\delta}{1 + \delta f_{t+T,t+T}}.$$

The effect of the LIBOR convention is to modify the drift of the forward rate. The following is a straightforward generalisation of equation (7.15). The drift of the forward rate is given in the two-period case by

$$E_t^Q\left(f_{t+1,t+2}\right) - f_{t,t+2}$$

$$= -\frac{1}{\delta}\text{cov}_t^Q\left(\delta f_{t+1,t+2}, \frac{1}{1 + \delta f_{t+1,t+1}}\frac{1}{1 + \delta f_{t+1,t+2}}\right)$$

$$\times \left(1 + \delta f_{t,t+1}\right)\left(1 + \delta f_{t,t+2}\right).$$

and in general for the T-maturity forward rate:

$$E_t^Q\left(f_{t+1,t+T}\right) - f_{t,t+T}$$

$$= -\frac{1}{\delta}\text{cov}_t^Q\left(\delta f_{t+1,t+T}, \frac{1}{1 + \delta f_{t+1,t+1}}\cdots\frac{1}{1 + \delta f_{t+1,t+T}}\right)$$

$$\times \left(1 + \delta f_{t,t+1}\right)\cdots\left(1 + \delta f_{t,t+T}\right).$$

Hence it follows that[51]

$$E_t^Q\left(f_{t+1,t+T}\right) - f_{t,t+T}$$

$$= f_{t,t+T}\frac{\delta f_{t,t+1}}{1 + \delta f_{t,t+1}}\text{cov}_t^Q\left(\ln f_{t+1,t+T}, \ln f_{t+1,t+1}\right)$$

$$+ \cdots + f_{t,t+T}\frac{\delta f_{t,t+T}}{1 + \delta f_{t,t+T}}\text{cov}_t^Q\left(\ln f_{t+1,t+T}, \ln f_{t+1,t+T}\right).$$

Finally, to obtain the drift of LIBOR in the Brace *et al.*(1996) model, we assume that the covariance structure is inter-temporally

---

[51] Note that this expression uses the fact that

$$\text{cov}_t^Q\left(\ln \delta f_{t+1,t+T}, \ln \delta f_{t+1,t+1}\right) = \text{cov}_t^Q\left(\ln f_{t+1,t+T}, \ln f_{t+1,t+1}\right).$$

stable. That is, we assume that $\text{cov}_t^Q \left(\ln f_{t+1,t+\tau}, \ln f_{t+1,t+T} \right)$ is a function of the forward maturities and is not dependent on t. Then we can write

$$\text{cov}_t^Q \left(\ln f_{t+1,t+1+\tau}, \ln f_{t+1,t+1+T} \right) = \sigma_{\tau,T},$$

where $\sigma_{\tau,T}$ is the covariance of the log τ-period forward LIBOR and the log T-period forward LIBOR. We can then write:

$$\frac{E_t^Q \left(f_{t+1,t+T} \right) - f_{t,t+T}}{f_{t,t+T}} = \frac{\delta f_{t,t+1}}{1 + \delta f_{t,t+1}} \sigma_{0,T-1} + \frac{\delta f_{t,t+2}}{1 + \delta f_{t,t+2}} \sigma_{1,T-1}$$
$$+ \cdots + \frac{\delta f_{t,t+T}}{1 + \delta f_{t,t+T}} \sigma_{T-1,T-1}. \qquad (7.19)$$

For example, when $t = 0$ and $T = 2$

$$\frac{E_t^Q \left(f_{t+1,t+2} \right) - f_{t,t+2}}{f_{t,t+2}} = \frac{\delta f_{t,t+1}}{1 + \delta f_{t,t+1}} \sigma_{0,1} + \frac{\delta f_{t,t+2}}{1 + \delta f_{t,t+2}} \sigma_{1,1}.$$

Equation (7.19) shows how to calculate the drift of the forward LIBORs under the period-by-period risk-neutral measure. It shows that the drift depends on a series of discounted covariances. One difficulty highlighted by the equation is that the drift is stochastic, since it depends on the future state-dependent forward LIBORs. This implies that in any impementation, it is difficult to produce a simple re-combining tree of rates. Also note that the spot LIBOR is not unconditionally lognormal, given the stochastic drift. For these reasons most implementations of the LIBOR market model use Monte Carlo simulation to compute interest-rate derivatives prices.

7.4   Conclusions

In this chapter we have introduced the topic of bond pricing in a rational expectations, pricing kernel model. We have used the no-arbitrage model to derive bond forward prices, the drift of bond forward prices, and the drift of interest rates. The LIBOR market model suggested by Brace et al.(1996) and Milterson et al.(1997), is an application of these basic ideas to the case where interest rates are defined on a LIBOR basis. We have derived the drift of LIBOR under the risk-neutral measure but have not investigated the pricing of interest-rate derivatives using the model. Readers

interested in pursuing this topic could look at Hull (2003) and
Bjork (2004).

7.5   Appendix

In this appendix, we present two technical results which are
required in the proof of the drift of forward rates. The first follows
from Taylor's theorem. The second is an implication of Stein's
lemma.

Lemma 7 (Covariances of Logarithms) *Taylor's series
expansion involves approximating the value of $g(x)$ around the
value $x = a$*

$$g(x) = g(a) + g'(a)(x-a) + \tfrac{1}{2}g''(a)\cdots$$

Now define $g(x) = \ln X$, then from Taylor's theorem, we can write

$$\ln X = \ln a + \frac{1}{a}(X-a) + \ldots$$

and similarly

$$\ln Y = \ln b + \frac{1}{b}(Y-b) + \ldots$$

Hence

$$\operatorname{cov}(\ln X, \ln Y) \approx \frac{1}{a}\frac{1}{b}\operatorname{cov}(X,Y)$$

$$\operatorname{cov}(X,Y) \approx ab\ \operatorname{cov}(\ln X, \ln Y)$$

with the first-order approximation.

Lemma 8 (Stein's Lemma for lognormal variables) *For
joint-normal variables x and y*

$$\operatorname{cov}[x, g(y)] = E[g'(y)]\operatorname{cov}(x,y).$$

Hence, if $x = \ln X$ and $y = \ln Y$, then

$$\operatorname{cov}\left[\ln X, \ln\left(\frac{1}{1+Y}\right)\right] = E\left(\frac{-Y}{1+Y}\right)\operatorname{cov}(\ln X, \ln Y).$$

Proof   Let $g\left(\ln Y\right) = \ln\left(\dfrac{1}{1+Y}\right)$

$$g'\left(\ln Y\right) = \frac{\mathrm{d}g}{\mathrm{d}\ln Y} = \frac{\mathrm{d}g}{\mathrm{d}Y} \times \frac{\mathrm{d}Y}{\mathrm{d}\ln Y}$$

$$= \frac{1}{\left(1+Y\right)^{-1}}\left(-1\right)\left(1+Y\right)^{-2} \times Y$$

$$= -\frac{Y}{1+Y}.$$

From Stein's lemma,

$$\mathrm{cov}\left[\ln X, \ln\left(\frac{1}{1+Y}\right)\right] = E\left(\frac{-Y}{1+Y}\right)\mathrm{cov}\left(\ln X, \ln Y\right).$$

∎

Exercises

7.1. What is the drift of the futures price of a bond under the risk-neutral measure? How does this differ from the drift of the forward price of a bond under the risk-neutral measure?

7.2. Show that

$$F_{t,t+1,t+n} = F_{t,t+1,t+2} F_{t,t+2,t+n},$$

and hence that

$$E_t^Q \left(\frac{1}{1+y_{t+1}} \frac{1}{1+f_{t+1,t+2}} \right) = \frac{1}{1+f_{t,t+1}} \frac{1}{1+f_{t,t+2}}.$$

7.3. In the case of the two-period forward, we show in (7.14) that the drift is

$$E_t^Q \left(f_{t+1,t+2} \right) - f_{t,t+2}$$
$$= -\text{cov}_t^Q \left(f_{t+1,t+2}, \frac{1}{1+y_{t+1}} \frac{1}{1+f_{t+1,t+2}} \right)$$
$$\times (1 + f_{t,t+1}) (1 + f_{t,t+2}).$$

Show that a similar relationship holds for the three-period forward

$$E_t^Q \left(f_{t+1,t+3} \right) - f_{t,t+3}$$
$$= -\text{cov}_t^Q \left(f_{t+1,t+3}, \frac{1}{1+y_{t+1}} \frac{1}{1+f_{t+1,t+2}} \frac{1}{1+f_{t+1,t+3}} \right)$$
$$\times (1 + f_{t,t+1}) (1 + f_{t,t+2}) (1 + f_{t,t+3}).$$

7.4. The drift of the two-period forward rate depends upon the term

$$\text{cov}_t^Q \left(f_{t+1,t+2}, \frac{1}{1+y_{t+1}} \frac{1}{1+f_{t+1,t+2}} \right).$$

Write down all the steps showing that this equals

$$f_{t,t+2} \frac{f_{t,t+1}}{1 + f_{t,t+1}} \operatorname{cov}_t^Q \left(\ln f_{t+1,t+2}, \ln f_{t+1,t+1} \right)$$

$$+ f_{t,t+2} \frac{f_{t,t+2}}{1 + f_{t,t+2}} \operatorname{cov}_t^Q \left(\ln f_{t,t+2}, \ln f_{t,t+2} \right).$$

7.5. In the LIBOR market model, the drift of the forward rate is the sum of a set of discounted covariances of the forward rates [see equation (7.19)]. Discuss the assumptions that have been made in deriving this result and their significance in the argument.

Appendix: Stein's lemma

Since Stein's lemma (1973) is crucial to pricing relationships derived in several chapters, a summary of Stein's lemma is shown in this appendix.

First define

$$h'(y) = \left(\frac{y - \mu_y}{\sigma_y^2}\right) f(y), \qquad (A.1)$$

where $f(y)$ is the normal density function. Note that (A.1) implies

$$h(y) = -f(y), \qquad (A.2)$$

since if

$$h(y) = -\frac{1}{\sigma_y \sqrt{2\pi}} e^{-\frac{1}{2}\left(\frac{y-\mu_y}{\sigma_y}\right)^2}$$

$$h'(y) = \frac{y - \mu_y}{\sigma_y^2} \frac{1}{\sigma_y \sqrt{2\pi}} e^{-\frac{1}{2}\left(\frac{y-\mu_y}{\sigma_y}\right)^2}$$

$$= \frac{y - \mu_y}{\sigma_y^2} f(y).$$

Lemma 9 (Integration by parts)

$$\int h'g = \int g'f$$

Proof

$$hg = \int (hg)' = \int [h'g + g'h] = \int h'g + \int g'h \qquad (A.3)$$

$$\implies \int h'g = \int (hg)' - \int g'h.$$

Now since

$$\int_a^b (hg)' = hg(b) - hg(a),$$

from (A.3)

$$\int h'g = hg\,(\infty) - hg\,(-\infty) - \int g'h$$

$$= h\,(\infty)\,g\,(\infty) - h\,(-\infty)\,g\,(-\infty) - \int g'h.$$

Given that $f\,(\infty) = f\,(-\infty) = 0$ then from (A.2) $h\,(\infty) = h\,(-\infty) = 0$. Then, if $g\,(y)$ is bounded, we get, using (A.2),

$$\int h'g = -\int g'h = \int g'f.$$

∎

Stein's lemma specifies the covariance of x and a function of y when x and y are a pair of bivariate normal variables as follows.

Lemma 10 (Stein's lemma)

$$\operatorname{cov}\,[x, g\,(y)] = E\,[g'\,(y)]\operatorname{cov}\,(x, y)$$

Proof Consider

$$E\,[xg\,(y)] = E\,(x)\,E\,[g\,(y)] + \operatorname{cov}\,[x, g\,(y)] \qquad (A.4)$$

Rewrite the LHS of (A.4) in terms of conditional expectations:

$$E\,[xg\,(y)] = E\,[g\,(y)\,E\,(x\,|\,y)]. \qquad (A.5)$$

Since x and y are joint-normal

$$x = a + by + \varepsilon \qquad (A.6)$$
$$E\,(x) = a + bE\,(y)$$
$$E\,(x\,|\,y) = a + by$$
$$= E\,(x) - bE\,(y) + by.$$

Hence (A.5) becomes

$$E\,[x\,g\,(y)] = E\,\{g\,(y)\,[\mu_x + b\,(y - \mu_y)]\}$$
$$= E\,[g\,(y)\,\mu_x] + bE\,[g\,(y)\,(y - \mu_y)].$$

Now substitute into LHS of (A.4):

$$E\left[g\left(y\right)\mu_x\right] + bE\left[g\left(y\right)\left(y - \mu_y\right)\right] = \mu_x E\left[g\left(y\right)\right] + \text{cov}\left(x,\ g\left(y\right)\right)$$

$$\text{cov}\left[x, g\left(y\right)\right] = bE\left[g\left(y\right)\left(y - \mu_y\right)\right]. \qquad (\text{A.7})$$

Since from bivariate normal regression in (A.6):

$$b = \frac{\text{cov}\left(x, y\right)}{\sigma_y^2},$$

so

$$\text{cov}\left[x,\ g\left(y\right)\right] = \text{cov}\left(x, y\right) E\left[g\left(y\right)\frac{\left(y - \mu_y\right)}{\sigma_y^2}\right]$$

$$= \text{cov}\left(x, y\right) \int g\left(y\right)\left(\frac{y - \mu_y}{\sigma_y^2}\right) f\left(y\right)\,\mathrm{d}y$$

$$= \text{cov}\left(x, y\right) \int g\left(y\right) h'\left(y\right)\,\mathrm{d}y. \qquad (\text{A.8})$$

Using lemma (9)

$$\text{cov}\left[x,\ g\left(y\right)\right] = \text{cov}\left(x, y\right) \int g'\left(y\right) f\left(y\right)\,\mathrm{d}y$$

$$= \text{cov}\left(x, y\right) E\left[g'\left(y\right)\right].$$

∎

BIBLIOGRAPHY

[1] Bernardo, A.E. and Ledoit, O. (2000). Gain, loss, and asset pricing. *Journal of Political Economy* **108**(1), 144–72.

[2] Bernoulli, D. (1954). Exposition of a new theory on the measurement of risk. *Econometrica*, 23–36.

[3] Bjork, T. (2004). *Arbitrage Theory in Continuous Time.* Oxford University Press.

[4] Black, F. and Scholes, M. (1973). The pricing of options and corporate liabilities. *Journal of Political Economy* **81**, 637–54.

[5] Camara, A. (2003). A generalization of the Brennan–Rubeinstein approach for the pricing of derivatives. *Journal of Finance* **53**(2), 805–19.

[6] Cochrane, J.H. (2001). *Asset Pricing.* Princeton University Press, NJ.

[7] Cochrane, J.H. and Saa-Requejo, J. (2000). Beyond arbitrage: Good-deal asset price bounds in incomplete markets. *Journal of Political Economy* **108**(1), 79–119.

[8] Copeland, T.E. and Western, J.F. (1983). Financial Theory and Corporate Policy. Addison-Wesley.

[9] Cox, J.C., Ingersoll, J.E. Jr and Ross, S.A. (1981). The relationship between forward prices and futures prices. *Journal of Financial Economics* **9**, 321–46.

[10] Cox, J.C., Ingersoll, J.E. Jr and Ross, S.A. (1985a). A theory of the term structure of interest rates. *Econometrica* **53**(2), 385–407.

[11] Cox, J.C., Ingersoll, J.E. and Ross, S.A. (1985b). An intertemporal general equilibrium model of asset prices. *Econometrica* **53**(2), 363–84.

[12] Cox, J.C. and Rubinstein, M. (1985). *Options Markets.* Prentice Hall, New York.

[13] Fama, E. and Miller, M. (1972). *Theory of Finance*, New York, Holt, Rinchart and Winston.

[14] Franke, G., Huang, J. and Stapleton, R. (2003). A two-dimensional risk-neutral valuation relationship for the

pricing of options, Working Paper, Lancaster University and Manchester University.

[15] Franke, G., Stapleton, R.C. and Subrahmanyam, M.G. (1998). Who buys and who sells options: the role of options in an economy with background risk. *Journal of Economic Theory* **82**(1), 89–109.

[16] Franke, G., Stapleton, R.C. and Subrahmanyam, M.G. (1999). When are options overpriced? The Black–Scholes model and alternative characteristics of the pricing kernel. *European Financial Review* **3**, 79–102.

[17] Gollier, C. (2000). *The Economics of Risk and Time.* Book, MIT Press, Cambridge, MA.

[18] Gollier, C. and Pratt, J. (1990). Risk vulnerability and the tempering effect of background risk. *Econometrica* **64**, 1109–23.

[19] Harrison, J.M. and Kreps, D.M. (1979). Martingales and arbitrage in multiperiod securities markets. *Journal of Economic Theory* **20**, 381–408.

[20] Heston, S.L. (1993). Invisible parameters in option prices. *Journal of Finance* **58**(3), 933–47.

[21] Huang, C.-F. and Litzenberger, R.H. (1988). *Foundations for Financial Economics.* North Holland, Amsterdam.

[22] Hull, J. (2003). *Options, Futures and Other Derivative Securities,* 5th edn. Prentice-Hall International, New York.

[23] Kimball, M.S. (1990). Precautionary saving in the small and in the large. *Econometrica* **58**, 53–73.

[24] Kimball, M.S. (1993). Standard risk aversion. *Econometrica* **61**, 589–611.

[25] LeRoy, S.F. and Werner, J. (2001). *Principles of Financial Economics.* Cambridge University Press, Cambridge.

[26] Merton, R.C. (1969). Lifetime portfolio selection under uncertainty: the continuous time case. *Review of Economics and Statistics* **51**, 247–57.

[27] Merton, R.C. (1973). Theory of rational option pricing. *Bell Journal of Economics and Management Science* **4**, 141–83.

[28] Milterson, K.R., Sandmann, K. and Sondermann, D. (1997). Closed form solutions for term structure derivatives with lognormal interest rates, *Journal of Finance* **52**(1), 409–30.

[29] Mood, A.M., Graybill, F.A. and Boes, D.C. (1974). *Introduction to the Theory of Statistics.* McGraw-Hill.

[30] Nachman, D.C. (1982). Preservation of 'more risk aversion' under expectations. *Journal of Economic Theory* **28**, 361–8.

[31] Pliska, S. (1997). *Introduction to Mathematical Finance.* Blackwell.

[32] Pratt, J.W. (1964). Risk aversion in the small and in the large with applications. *Econometrica* **32**, 122–36.

[33] Rubinstein, M. (1976). The valuation of uncertain income streams and the pricing of options. *Bell Journal of Economics and Management Science* **7**, 407–25.

[34] Rubinstein, M. (1983). Displaced diffusion option pricing. *Journal of Finance* **38**, 213–17.

[35] Satchel, S.E., Stapleton, R.C. and Subrahmanyam, M.G. (1997). The pricing of marked to market contingent claims in a no-arbitrage economy. *Australian Journal of Management* **22**(1), 1–20.

[36] Stapleton, R.C. (1980). The language of MPT, the market model, the diagonal model and the CAPM. *Investment Analysts Journal* **58**, 15–17.

[37] Stapleton, R.C. and Subrahmanyam, M.G. (1978). A multiperiod equilibrium asset pricing model. *Econometrica* **46**(5), 1077–96.

[38] Stein, C. (1973). Estimation of the mean of a multivariate normal distribution. *Proceedings of the Prague Symposium on Asymptotic Statistics*, September, 345–81.

[39] Stuart, A. and Ord, J.K. (1993). Kendall's advanced theory of statistics (Vol. 1), *Distribution Theory.* John Wiley & Sons Inc, New York.

[40] Weil, P. (1992). Equilibrium asset prices with undiversifiable labor income risk. *Journal of Economic Dynamics and Control* **16**, 769–90.

[41] Williams, D. (1991). *Probability with Martingales.* Cambridge University Press, Cambridge.

INDEX